LF

Industrial and business forecasting methods

Forecasting in business is like sex in society, we have to have it, we cannot get along without it; everyone is doing it, one way or the other, but nobody is sure he is doing it the best way.

G.W. Plossl, *Manufacturing Control – The Last Frontier for Profits*

Industrial and business forecasting methods

A practical guide to exponential smoothing and curve fitting

COLIN D LEWIS

Professor of Operations Management
University of Aston

Butterworth Scientific
London Boston Sydney Wellington Durban Toronto

First published 1982

© Butterworth & Co (Publishers) Ltd, 1982

British Library Cataloguing in Publication Data

Lewis, C.D.
   Industrial and business forecasting
   methods.
   1. Forecasting
   I. Title
   003   CB158

   ISBN 0-408-00559-9

Typeset by Scribe Design, Gillingham, Kent
Printed in England by The Camelot Press Ltd., Southampton

Preface

This book is aimed quite simply at those who possess time-series data which they wish to forecast.

Forecasts are interpreted as being the result of extrapolating the past into the future. It is assumed that forecasts are derived from an objective series of calculations or computations involving data, whereas subjective estimates of future values are termed 'predictions'. Forecasts are, therefore, unbiased estimates of future data values. As such they can and should be modified if subjective predictions confidently indicate that an unbiased estimate is unlikely to be an effective estimate of what will occur. For example, given that it is known that a major customer is going to suffer a strike next month, it is obviously quite pointless to assume that a forecast based on the last nine months of that customer's demand is likely to be at all accurate.

Since the early sixties, the proportion of industrial and business organizations using forecasting techniques has increased steadily, such that in 1977[1] it was established that forecasting techniques were used by 88% of the 500 largest industrial companies in the USA. Moreover, it was also established that no other single family of techniques was used as much as forecasting.

Along with the growth of the use of forecasting techniques, there has been a parallel growth in the variety of forecasting models on offer from the theorists. In spite of this increasingly wide range of available forecasting models, it has also become apparent that the choice of forecasting model actually used follow a typical *Pareto* relationship, such that 20% of the models available are used in 80% of practical forecasting applications and the remaining 80% of models are used in only 20% of applications. It is with the former which this book is exclusively concerned.

The two principal forecasting model types (and their derivatives) which feature in the vast majority of forecasting applications are exponential smoothing and regression (including curve fitting). The main reasons for the undoubted popularity of these methods are:

(i)   their relative simplicity;
(ii) their economy in computational and storage terms;

(iii) the fact they are automatic, in model identification terms, such that forecasts can be produced without subjective intervention;

(iv) they have been extensively used for over twenty years.

The first section of this book deals with exponential smoothing methods which are generally recognized as falling into the *short-term* forecasting area. These forecasting techniques are associated mainly with data based on a time period of less than one year, i.e. demand per month, sales per quarter, etc.

The second section of the book deals with regression and curve fitting methods which are generally recognized as falling into the *medium-term* forecasting area and, although more usually associated with yearly-based data, can often be used for data based on shorter time periods if no seasonality is present.

As, in practice, most forecasting is done using a computer (or programmable calculator) the text of this book is supported by flow diagrams and worked tables to assist the reader in programming and debugging forecasting programs designed to suit his or her own situations.

C.D. Lewis
Solihull

1. LEDBETTER, W.N. and COX, J.F. (1977) 'Operations research in production management: an investigation of past and present utilization', *Production and Inventory Management*, 18, 84

Acknowledgements

I am indebted to Dr Keith Yeomans for his comments and criticism, to Jenny Hipkiss for her fast and accurate typing, to Vivienne Perks for her assistance in sorting out my programming problems, and to my family for allowing me to cover our dining-room table with books, papers, computer printouts, etc. for months on end; other than at Sunday lunchtime.

C.D.L.

Contents

Preface
Acknowledgements

Short-term forecasting (exponential smoothing methods)

Introduction

Short-term forecasting is generally concerned with:

(i) data associated with a time period of less than one year (i.e. calendar months, accounting periods in a year — usually 12 or 13, quarters, weeks, etc.);

(ii) situations where forecasts are associated with a particular item and for which forecasts are updated every time period;

(iii) situations where forecasts are required for a large number of items;

(iv) situations where the forecasts produced for a particular item or product and are used on a period to period basis to: (a) analyse demand and to assess appropriate inventory levels and production schedules, and (b) analyse sales to help assess cash flows and to ascertain marketing procedures.

It is apparent that for these types of application the most appropriate forecasting model (or series of models) needs to be:

(i) cheap to operate — in terms of implementation, routine updating and storage requirement costs;

(ii) flexible and hence able to offer a variety of different, but closely related, model types suitable for a wide variety of items and situations for which forecasts could be required;

(iii) largely automatic, such that a minimum of manual interruption is necessary;

(iv) well proven, and hence, readily available in both the literature and computer software.

The range of forecasting models based on the exponentially weighted average (collectively referred to as exponential smoothing methods), which were introduced in the early 1960's, has been shown to fulfil most of the above requirements.

The superiority of exponential smoothing methods over the traditional moving average concept is such that today most manufacturing organizations of any size use them and no industrial or business computer software is complete without them.

In Section 1, Chapter 1 develops the concept of the simple exponentially weighted average on which all smoothing models are based and

3

Chapter 2 is concerned with the more sophisticated variants of the basic model, which are necessary for growth and seasonal situations. Chapter 3 examines various measures of dispersion of forecasting errors and Chapter 4 the smoothing techniques developed specifically for the automatic monitoring of short-term forecasts. Chapter 5 examines the possibilities of adaptive forecasting models and Chapter 6, although not specifically based on exponential smoothing methods, examines the use of autocorrelation analysis in identifying data characteristics, a necessary pre-requisite for determining the appropriate type of forecasting model.

The forecasting methods included within this book must necessarily be expressed in mathematical terms. In order not to 'frighten off' the layman this Introduction will be used to present the ideas of symbolic representation of variables and the use of algebraic equations. Anyone able to understand these simple concepts will have no difficulty in following the material presented.

As an example, let us take a naive forecasting scheme which says 'Let the forecast for next month's expected demand be equal to the demand that occurred this month'. This could be written as:

$$\text{FORECAST}_{\text{next month}} \text{ EQUALS DEMAND}_{\text{this month}}$$

Using the first letters of *forecast* and *demand* as symbols representing those variables respectively, and introducing an equals (=) sign, this forecasting scheme could be rewritten as:

$$f_{\text{next month}} = d_{\text{this month}}$$

To complete the 'tidying up' of this equation we need to simplify and generalize the subscripts *next month* and *this month*. The simplest way of doing this is to work with months (or, in other situations, accounting periods, weeks or even days) as our period of time, and to refer all time to current (or present) time. Thus if we regard present time as t, then future time can be considered positive with respect to t (i.e. as $t + 1$, $t + 2$, etc.) and past time can be considered as negative (i.e. $t - 1$, $t - 2$, etc.). Having developed a method of subscripting to indicate time we can now rewrite our naive forecasting scheme as a generalized algebraic equation of the form:

$$f_{t+1} = d_t \tag{0.1}$$

Evidence of how much simpler is such symbolic representation, compared with a written statement, can be seen by considering a more practical forecasting scheme which predicts that 'Next month's expected demand will be equal to the arithmetic average of the last six months' demand or sales figures'. This lengthy statement can be written very briefly in equation form as:

$$f_{t+1} = {}^1/_6 \sum_{i=t}^{t-5} d_i \qquad (0.2)$$

where the summation sign

$$\sum_{i=t}^{t-5}$$

means in this situation the sum of the values of d_i from i equals t up to and including $t-5$ (i.e. $t, t-1, t-2, t-3, t-4$ and $t-5$). Expanding the summation sign this equation would appear as:

$$f_{t+1} = {}^1/_6(d_t + d_{t-1} + d_{t-2} + d_{t-3} + d_{t-4} + d_{t-5}) \qquad (0.3)$$

which would be an alternative form of equation (0.2).

This concludes the introduction to the concepts of symbolic representation and algebraic equations. The material presented in this book is deliberately chosen not to be more complicated than this.

Chapter 1

Forecasting for stationary situations

A stationary situation is one in which, although observed values fluctuate from one time period to the next, the average value remains steady over a reasonably long period of time. To illustrate this, Fig. 1.1 shows a series of demand values plotted against time. It can be seen that the average value per month over the one-year period is about 100 items per month, and that this average figure is neither increasing nor declining significantly with time. This is a typical stationary situation,

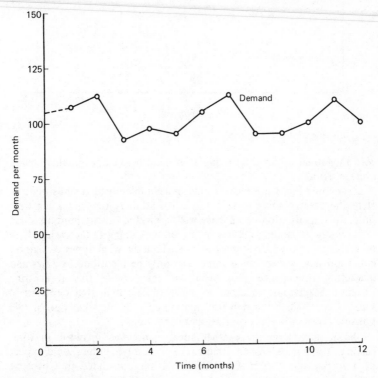

Fig. 1.1 Typical stationary situation

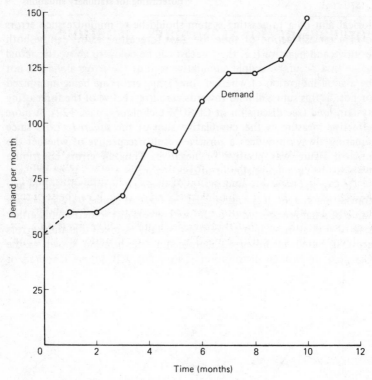

Fig. 1.2 Non-stationary situation

with individual values fluctuating above and below a reasonably steady average figure.

Examining Fig. 1.2, however, reveals a completely different situation. Here the average value is definitely not stationary but increasing with time. Such a situation could arise with a product maintaining its share of a rapidly expanding market or a product gaining an increasing share of a static (or even declining) market. Exactly what types of market condition have caused such values can only be identified by sales and marketing intelligence, but whatever the reason, this forecasting situation is obviously a more complicated one than that depicted in Fig. 1.1 and will be dealt with separately in Chapter 2 as one of two possible types of linear, non-stationary situations.

Before discussing the mathematical techniques involved in forecasting, it might be best to discuss initially just what one should expect of a forecasting system. First, it should be appreciated that because one's forecasts are based on past information, there will always be some degree of forecasting error. Accepting this, it is apparent that the most logical aim of a forecasting system should be to minimize such errors over a longish period of time. Because forecasting errors can be both positive and negative (i.e. the forecast can be below or above the actual value that occurs) a simple cumulative sum of the errors alone will not be a good indication of whether forecasting errors are being minimized or not, as this sum will tend towards zero irrespective of the forecasting system used (see discussion of CUSUM techniques, page 122). A more effective measure is the cumulative sum of the *squared* errors since squaring always produces a positive result irrespective of whether the original figure was positive or negative. Thus all errors contribute towards the cumulative sum of squared errors.

Once it has been accepted that some degree of error is present in any forecasting system, it is evident that the forecast can be only an average value of what is expected to occur, with errors distributed evenly either side of that average. In practice it is generally assumed that these errors are distributed according to a probability distribution known as the Gaussian or Normal distribution. This point will not be laboured or

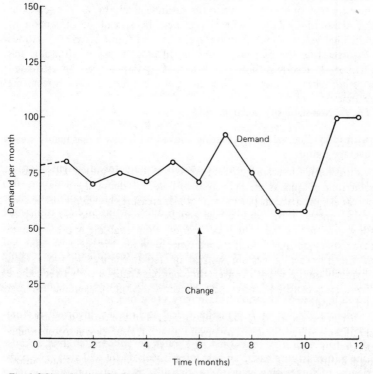

Fig. 1.3 Situation in which the standard deviation suddenly increases

explained further here except to say that the assumption is reasonably true so long as the value of the average per time period is not too low, which is generally true of the items we are concerned with in short-term forecasting if this average value is generally greater than ten.

Assuming that errors are distributed normally, we need some measure of the spread or the degree of dispersion of errors around the average. The usual measure of dispersion is known as the *standard deviation,* represented universally by the Greek symbol σ, and Fig. 1.3 indicates a situation in which the standard deviation suddenly increases owing to a change in the underlying data pattern.

For this situation the forecast would not change appreciably as the average value remains at approximately 75 per month, even after the change. However, it is evident that the spread of values, or variation, has changed after the sixth month and this change, in an efficient forecasting system, would be noted by a change in the value of the standard deviation σ.

Thus there are *two* basic parameters we wish to estimate in any forecasting system. The first is the actual forecast which predicts what the expected or average value in the future is likely to be. The second is the standard deviation which measures the spread or dispersion of individual values about that average. Chapters 1 and 2 present methods of forecasting the expected value in different types of situation and Chapter 3 describes how the standard deviation can be estimated together with the methods of evaluating other measures of forecasting accuracy.

Forecasting time period

A short-term forecasting system treats the total of individual values in each time period as a single item of data, i.e. demand per day, sales per week, production per month, etc. Increasing the length of the time period increases the sample size and hence reduces the variability of successive individual values per period thus enabling more accurate forecasts to be made. At the same time, however, the speed of response of the forecasting system to real or actual changes in the data is obviously reduced with longer time periods. A balance between these two effects can be achieved only by the selection of a suitable forecast time period.

It can be shown that the minimum value of the forecast time period should be of a duration to ensure that at least one non-zero value occurs in two time periods, that is that there is a 50 per cent probability that a non-zero value will occur during one time period. This is a minimum; overall considerations may require a longer interval.

This criterion of having one non-zero value occurring within two periods is normally met for industrial and business data if the time period is greater than or equal to one week, and a calendar month (or more practically a planning or accounting period of that order) is most typical.

The number of time periods ahead for which forecasts are produced is known as the forecast *horizon*.

The moving or rolling average*

One traditional method of forecasting the future average expected value per time period is to average the past individual values over the last n time periods. Such a moving average (m_t) has already been discussed in the Introduction see page 5, and could be defined as

$$m_t = \frac{1}{n} \sum_{i=t}^{t-n+1} d_i \qquad (1.1)$$

or, alternatively,

$$m_t = m_{t-1} + \frac{1}{n}(d_t - d_{t-n}) \qquad (1.2)$$

This latter version simply means that we put the current value of the moving average as being equal to the immediate past value plus $1/n$ times the current value less the value now n periods old.

Having calculated m_t for a stationary situation this then becomes the forecast of what one expects to occur, not only in the next time period but for any future time period.

This does not mean, however, that if one makes a forecast, say, for six months hence, this estimate cannot be modified next month, when an additional month's information can be used to improve the estimate, which is now only five months away. This concept may be slightly difficult to follow but corresponds very much with planning schedules, which are definite for the first and second months but only tentative for the third and fourth months. The tentative plans then become definite at the next two-monthly review in the same way that a vague forecast can become more definite as further information is received as time progresses.

The moving average does, however, in practice have several drawbacks which are discussed here:

*Known to latter-day, purist statisticians as an autoregressive process.

(i) Starting a moving average. When beginning the calculation of a moving average from new data, because it is necessary to have individual values available for the previous $n-1$ periods, no true forecast can be made until at least n periods have passed.

(ii) With a moving average, all the data included within the average are 'weighted' equally and data too old to be included are obviously given zero weighting. The weight of an item indicates the proportion of its value that an item contributes to an average, which in the case of the moving average is $1/n$ for all items included in the average, and zero for those not included.

A criticism of a method of equal weighting is that more recent data should be more important than older data and should, therefore, be weighted more highly.

A method using unequal weights could be proposed to resolve this feature, and two possible weighted averages based on either fractional or decimal concepts are shown here as equations (1.3) and (1.4) respectively. Note that in both the sum of the weights is *one*; this, by definition, is always necessary of a true average.

$$m_t = \tfrac{1}{2}d_t + \tfrac{1}{4}d_{t-1} + \tfrac{3}{16}d_{t-2} + \tfrac{1}{16}d_{t-3} \tag{1.3}$$

or

$$m_t = 0.4d_t + 0.3d_{t-1} + 0.2d_{t-2} + 0.1d_{t-3} \tag{1.4}$$

(iii) With a moving average, the amount of past data that must be retained can become excessive. A six-period moving average has been discussed here but, in practice, to obtain an average which is not excessively sensitive, one can require data from up to 20 periods.

(iv) As the sensitivity or the speed of response of a moving average is inversely proportional to n, the number of time periods included in the average, it is difficult to change this sensitivity since it is also most difficult to change the value of n, as already illustrated by the initializing-average situation.

Most of the disadvantages presented by the moving average can be overcome by a moving average of a special type in which the weighting series is exponential.

The exponentially weighted average*

Suppose that, instead of one of the weighting systems used previously, it is proposed to use a series of weights whose values decrease *exponentially* with time.

*Referred to in more recent, advanced statistical texts — most confusingly — as a 'moving average' process.

This series would be defined as

$$\alpha + \alpha(1 - \alpha) + \alpha(1 - \alpha)^2 + \alpha(1 - \alpha)^3 \ldots + \alpha(1 - \alpha)^n$$

For a true average this series must sum to one and this can be shown to be true if α lies between zero and one. For instance if $\alpha = 0.2$ we obtain this series

$$0.200 + 0.160 + 0.128 + 0.102 + 0.082, \text{etc.},$$

which can be seen not only to be approaching a sum of unity, but also to have weights which decrease with age.

Using an exponential weighting series, an exponentially weighted average u_t would be given by

$$u_t = \alpha d_t + \alpha(1 - \alpha)d_{t-1} + \alpha(1 - \alpha)^2 d_{t-2} + \alpha(1 - \alpha)^3 d_{t-3} + \ldots (1.5)$$

which could be written alternatively as

$$u_t = \alpha d_t + (1 - \alpha)[\alpha d_{t-1} + \alpha(1 - \alpha)d_{t-2} + \alpha(1 - \alpha)^2 d_{t-3} + \ldots (1.6)$$

Transcribing u_t, as defined by (1.5), into u_{t-1} simply by subtracting one from all subscripts we obtain

$$u_{t-1} = \alpha d_{t-1} + \alpha(1 - \alpha)d_{t-2} + \alpha(1 - \alpha)^2 d_{t-3} + \alpha(1 - \alpha)^3 d_{t-4} + \ldots (1.7)$$

and u_{t-1} is exactly the same as all that which appears in the square bracket in equation (1.6). Thus, substituting u_{t-1} for this we obtain

$$u_t = \alpha d_t + (1 - \alpha)u_{t-1} \qquad (1.8)$$

and this is the basic equation defining a simple, exponentially weighted average[1], from which all exponential smoothing models derive.

The exponentially weighted average's advantages over the traditional moving average are respectively as follows:

(i) When beginning a forecast based on an exponentially weighted average, once an initial estimate has been made, further forecasts can be calculated immediately fresh data are available. There is no need for a special initializing procedure as with the moving average.

(ii) With an exponentially weighted average, the values of the weights decrease with time and there is no sudden cut-off point at which data are excluded as with the moving average.

(iii) Very little past data need to be retained for the calculation of the exponentially weighted average u_t, the only two values necessary being the past value of the average (u_{t-1}) and the current value (d_t).

As a means of comparison, it can be shown that for equivalent moving and exponentially weighted averages with the same 'average age of data' or sensitivity

$$\frac{n-1}{2} = \frac{1-\alpha}{\alpha} \tag{1.9}$$

Typical values of α used in industrial and business forecasting lie between 0.05 and 0.3, which means that the corresponding number of time periods that a moving average of similar sensitivity would require would be as follows

α	n
0.05	39
0.1	19
0.2	9
0.3	5.66 i.e. 6

Thus when using a value of α equal to 0.1, which is about the most popular value used in practice, an equivalent moving average would require data from 18 time periods to be stored permanently, and this is obviously generally impracticable.

(iv) The sensitivity of the exponentially weighted average can be altered at any time to suit the forecasting situation simply by changing the value of α. The higher the value of α the more sensitive the average becomes, and the lower the value of α the more stable it becomes. In practice it is not usual to use a value of below 0.05 and it is generally recommended that a value above 0.3 should not be used. This latter recommendation is made because there is some evidence to suggest that if such a high value were thought to be desirable, the assumption that the situations under consideration were stationary is most likely invalid. In such a situation the simple exponentially weighted average described in this chapter should not be used, but should be replaced by one of the models designed to fit such non-stationary cases, as described in Chapter 2. In spite of these comments, however, it is only fair to point out that values of α higher than 0.3 are used not infrequently; although whether such values are chosen with a full knowledge of the implications involved is open to doubt.

Evaluation of forecasts based on simple exponentially weighted averages

Whilst, in practice, most forecasts based on exponentially weighted averages are evaluated by some form of automatic computation, sometimes situations do arise where it is more convenient or more cost effective to perform the necessary calculations manually. This can be done using either a simple calculator or the Nomogram shown in Fig. 1.4. Essentially this Nomogram consists of three identical linear scales. At the left is the past forecast (u_{t-1}) scale and on the right the current data value (d_t) scale, both of which are linear and can be scaled to suit particular situations. Between these two scales are the current forecast

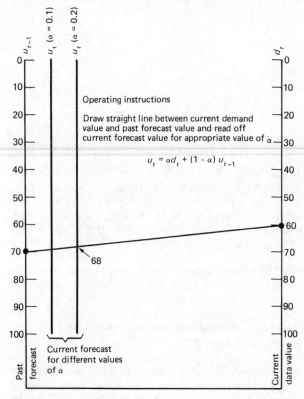

Fig. 1.4 Nomogram for calculating forecasts based on simple exponentially weighted averages

(u_t) scales for different values of α, the exponential smoothing constant. The positioning of these current forecast scales is quite simple. If $\alpha = 0.1$ the current forecast scale is placed one-tenth of the distance between the two outer scales away from the past forecast scale (and hence nine-tenths of that distance from the demand scale). Other positionings can be obtained for different values of α using this simple proportioning procedure and could be tabulated as in Table 1.1.

TABLE 1.1. Positioning of u_t scale

α	Distance from u_{t-1}	Distance from d_t
0.1	$\dfrac{1}{10}$	$\dfrac{9}{10}$
0.15	$\dfrac{3}{20}$	$\dfrac{17}{20}$
0.20	$\dfrac{1}{5}$	$\dfrac{4}{5}$
0.33	$\dfrac{1}{3}$	$\dfrac{2}{3}$
0.50	$\dfrac{1}{2}$	$\dfrac{1}{2}$

The exponentially weighted average Nomogram is used by drawing a straight line between the designated values of past forecast (u_{t-1}) and current value (d_t) and reading off the corresponding value of the forecast (u_t) on the scale appropriate to the value of α being used.

Thus, if $d_t = 60$ and $u_{t-1} = 70$, for a value of $\alpha = 0.2$, u_t can be read off as 68 units. This corresponds exactly with

$$u_t = (0.2 \times 60) + (0.8 \times 70)$$
$$= 12 + 56 = 68$$

Automatic methods of evaluating forecasts based on exponentially weighted averages

The calculations involved in evaluating forecasts based on the exponentially weighted average as defined by equation (1.8) are so simple, a discussion of how such calculations should be done hardly needs mentioning. However, a more compact form of equation (1.8) can be achieved by the realization that $(d_t - u_{t-1})$ represents the current value of the forecasting error e_t such that equation (1.8) could become

$$u_t = u_{t-1} + \alpha(d_t - u_{t-1}) \qquad (1.10)$$

and hence

$$u_t = u_{t-1} + \alpha e_t \qquad (1.11)$$

which many readers will recognize as being similar to a simple servo-mechanism system with proportional feedback. This form of the equation is used in Appendix A, a flow chart indicating the order and associated logic of calculations used to evaluate forecasts based on simple exponentially weighted averages.

Rounding and integer forecasts

If integer forecasts are required, which is often the case in industry and business, some form of rounding of the forecast value is frequently necessary.

The simplest rounding procedure, which is very nearly unbiased, is to add 0.5 to the value of the forecast and then take the integer part as the result. This ensures that 0.1, 0.2, 0.3 and 0.4 are rounded down and 0.5, 0.6, 0.7, 0.8 and 0.9 rounded up. Strictly speaking, such an approach is slightly biased since 0.5 should logically be rounded up and down with equal frequency, which, for those readers interested, can be achieved by rounding 0.5 consistently to the nearest *even* number.

Table 1.2 indicates a typical forecasting schedule for some monthly demand data where integer forecasts based on an exponentially weighted average have been evaluated. In Table 1.2 the value of the exponential smooth constant α has been chosen as 0.2. In the majority of practical applications α is either chosen to be 0.1 or 0.2 but some computer packages offer the user the option of searching for the optimal value of α on a criterion of minimizing, say, the sum of squared errors. For a series as short as in Table 1.2. however, the choice of the initial estimate of the forecast is often a more decisive factor.

Exponentially weighted averages have replaced moving averages as the predominant method used in short-term forecasting *not* because they produce better forecasts but essentially because they are computationally far simpler and also much more flexible[2]. Thus the basic exponential smoothing model can be further developed to cope with growth, seasonality and many other aspects of a comprehensive short-term forecasting system as will be evidenced by the reader in the following chapters.

References

1   HOLT, C.C. (1957) 'Forecasting seasonal and trends by exponentially weighted moving averages', *Naval Research Memorandum* No. 52
2   LEWIS, C.D. (1978) 'The versatility of the exponential smoother's portfolio of skills', *Production and Inventory Management*, 19, 53

TABLE 1.2. Typical forecasting schedule ($\alpha = 0.2$)

		Jan.	Feb.	Mar.	Apr.	May	June	July	Aug.	Sept.	Oct.	Nov.	Dec.	Jan.
This month's demand	d_t	60	70	55	80	90	65	70	75	60	80	90	100	95
Last month's forecast for this month	u_{t-1}	70*	68	68	65	68	72	71	71	72	70	72	76	81
$\alpha \times$ this month's demand	αd_t	12.0	14.0	11.0	16.0	18.0	13.0	14.0	15.0	12.0	16.0	18.0	20.0	19.0
$(1-\alpha) \times$ last month's forecast for this month	$(1-\alpha)u_{t-1}$	56.0	54.4	54.4	52.0	54.4	57.6	56.8	56.8	57.6	56.0	57.6	60.8	64.8
This month's forecast for next month (rounded)	$u_t = \alpha d_t + (1-\alpha)u_{t-1}$	68	68	65	68	72	71	71	72	70	72	76	81	84
This month's forecasting error	$e_t = d_t - u_{t-1}$	-10	2	-13	15	22	-7	-1	4	-12	10	18	24	14
Cumulative sum of squared errors	Σe_t^2	100	104	273	498	982	1031	1032	1048	1192	1292	1616	2192	2388

*Estimate based on sales intelligence.

Exercise

Using the data of Table 1.2 and the same initial assumption that $u_{t-1} = 70$, for $\alpha = 0.1$, 0.3 and 0.4 show that the sums of squared errors for the thirteen months are respectively 2615, 2357 and 2212. The reason that the optimal value of α is high is due to the increase in demand from October onwards.

Chapter 2

Forecasting for non-stationary situations–linear and seasonal variations

In Chapter 1 the various forecasting methods available for use in stationary situations, in which the average was assumed to be reasonably constant, were discussed. This chapter will be concerned with non-stationary situations in which the average value definitely does not remain constant, but varies with time.

This variation of the average with time is known as a 'trend' and trends can vary in character and type.

(i) Character of trends

(a) Linear trends

A linear trend is one in which the average value either increases or decreases linearly with time. A product with a linearly increasing trend could be typified by a new product with ever-increasing sales, or by a product in an expanding market retaining its percentage of that market.

A product with a linearly decreasing trend could be typified by a product rapidly becoming obsolete.

(b) Seasonal trends

A seasonal trend is one in which the average varies in a cyclical fashion in sympathy with some imposed time cycle. In most practical situations, this time cycle is invariably a yearly one in which the average in some months is up, compared with the overall monthly average, and in some months is down. Fashion goods such as clothes and shoes are naturally subject to such seasonal trends, but a large section of this country's engineering industry is similarly affected via the sales of cars, which decline with the approach of winter and increase in the spring.

(c) Combined linear and seasonal trends

As the name indicates, this type of trend is a direct combination of the two already mentioned. A good example of this can be seen in the

20

bookings for airline seats. The increasing use of air transport over the years provides the linear element of the trend and the seasonal pattern of travel within each year (as influenced by peak demands during the Christmas, Easter and summer holidays) provides the seasonal element, based on an annual time cycle.

(ii) Types of trends

(A) Additive trends

As well as having certain characteristics, trends can also be distinguished by their mathematical type. An additive type of trend is one in which an approximately regular amount is added to or subtracted from each consecutive average value, as influenced by the character of the trend. For instance, with a linear additive trend an average increase in demand of ten items for each consecutive month might be expected.

(B) Ratio trends (sometimes known as multiplicative trends)

A trend of a ratio type is subject to a percentage increase or decrease, as influenced by the character of the trend. Thus, the demand for an item with an increasing linear ratio trend might be expected to increase at, say, 2 per cent per month.

(C) Combined additive and ratio trends

This type of trend, which is of course a direct combination of the two already mentioned, tends to be rather complicated to analyse mathematically and is usually dealt with as one or the other.

When describing any demand trend it is necessary to describe both its type and character. The more usual trends for which relatively simple forecasting models have been developed are:

(aA) Linear additive trend

A product subject to this kind of trend would have an average value increasing (or decreasing) by an approximately fixed quantity each time period. Figure 2.1 shows such a situation, which is distinguished from a linear ratio trend case (Fig. 2.2) by the fact that, although the average value is increasing, the spread or variation of individual values about that average remains virtually constant.

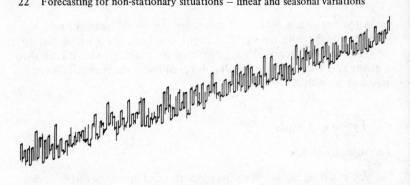

Fig. 2.1 Demand pattern subject to linear additive trend (aA)

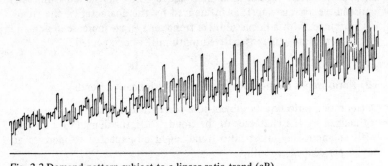

Fig. 2.2 Demand pattern subject to a linear ratio trend (aB)

(aB) Linear ratio trend

A product subject to a linear ratio trend would either increase (or decrease) its average value by an approximately fixed percentage with each successive time period. Figure 2.2 illustrates such a situation from which it can be seen that not only does the average value increase with time, but so also does the spread or variation of individual values about that average.

(cA) Combined linear and seasonal additive trend*

This type of trend also covers the situation of the pure seasonal trend with no linear element. Generally, however, models dealing with seasonal trends tend also to accept the possible influence of some linear element. A linear and seasonal additive trend situation is shown in Fig. 2.3. Note the two annual peaks being repeated year by year.

*Strictly interpreted, all seasonal models are ratio models and, in this case it is only the linear element which is additive.

Fig. 2.3 Demand pattern subject to both a linear and a seasonal additive trend (cA)

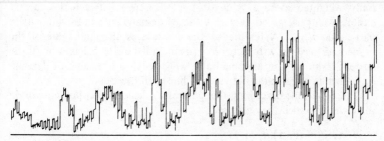

Fig. 2.4 Demand pattern subject to a seasonal ratio trend (cB)

(cB) Combined linear and seasonal ratio trend

This type of trend also covers the situation of the pure seasonal ratio trend with no linear element, an example of which is illustrated in Fig. 2.4. As with the combined linear and seasonal additive trend model, however, the analytical treatment of this type of trend always accepts the possible influence of some linear element in the trend.

The different trend types and characters more likely to occur in an industrial situation having been discussed*, the forecasting models developed specifically for such trends as aA, aB, cA and cB will now be detailed. For the casual reader, a summary of the methods used in non-stationary situations is given at the end of the chapter.

*For methods of trend identification see Chapter 6.

(aA) Linear additive trend forecasting models

When dealing with a linear additive trend model, it is assumed that the underlying process generating d_t has an average which changes linearly with time: thus

$$d_t = \mu + \lambda t + \epsilon_t \tag{2.0}$$

where μ is the process average, λ is the process growth rate, and ϵ_t is a random error with zero mean.

Several models have been proposed to meet this situation so each of these will be described in turn and some comparisons between the methods will be indicated.

(i) Holt's method

The method proposed by Holt[5] is based on estimating λ, the factor which measures the degree of linear growth (or decline) with time. This growth factor λ is estimated by b_t, which is calculated as the exponentially weighted average value of the difference between the current exponentially weighted average value of demand u_t and the immediate past value u_{t-1}. A feature of the method is that the value of the immediate past growth factor b_{t-1} is included in the calculation of the current value of the exponentially weighted average value of demand u_t, and thus updates the old value in line with the trend.

The equations describing this part of the calculation process are, in the order in which they are used,

$$u_t = A d_t + (1-A)(u_{t-1} + b_{t-1}) \tag{2.1}$$

and

$$b_t = B(u_t - u_{t-1}) + (1-B)b_{t-1} \tag{2.2}$$

where B also lies between zero and one, like A.

To estimate likely future values with any type of trend model, it is necessary to make specific reference to the period for which the forecast is being considered. Throughout this chapter, we shall consider that the forecast being calculated is for the period τ time periods ahead, that is at time $(t + \tau)$.

In Holt's model, having estimated the growth (or decline) factor b_t, a forecast for any period τ periods ahead, i.e. $f_{t+\tau}$, can be evaluated simply by adding to the estimate of what the average is at the current time (u_t), the expected increase due to the growth factor b_t and the number of time periods this is assumed to operate for, namely for τ periods. Thus

$$f_{t+T} = u_t + b_t \tau \tag{2.3}$$

I.C.I.[6], who in 1964 advocated the use of Holt's method, recommended values for A and B of 0.1 and 0.01 respectively. One of the disadvantages of Holt's method is that it is a two-parameter system (i.e. values for both A and B must be arbitrarily chosen).

(ii) Holt's method with Muir's modification

Muir[7] has shown that the value of the growth factor b_t evaluated using equation (2.2) is the least squares estimate of the true growth factor λ or, in other words, that estimate which minimizes the sum of the squared errors from the true demand process as defined by equation (2.0). Muir shows that if forecasts have been made for a reasonably long period of time (theoretically infinitely long) then, if

$$u_t = Ad_t + (1 - A)u_{t-1} \tag{2.4}$$

and b_t is calculated using equation (2.2), an unbiased estimate of the expected value τ periods ahead is given by

$$f_{t+\tau} = u_t + b_t\left(\frac{1}{A} + \tau - 1\right) \tag{2.5}$$

(iii) Brown's double smoothing method

This method of Brown's[2] accepts that, after initial transients have died down, a simple exponentially weighted average (equation (1.8)) will always lag behind a linear trend by an amount given by

$$\text{lag} = \frac{1 - \alpha}{\alpha}\lambda$$

where λ is the slope of the process trend as defined by equation (2.0).
Brown has also shown that a double exponentially weighted average $\bar{u}_t$, defined as

$$\bar{u}_t = \alpha u_t + (1 - \alpha)\bar{u}_{t-1} \tag{2.6}$$

will, after transients have died down, also lag behind the primary smoothed average u_t by the same amount as u_t lags behind d_t (see Fig. 2.5). Thus an estimate for the current value of d_t could be given as

$$f_t = u_t + (u_t - \bar{u}_t)$$

i.e. $\tag{2.7}$

$$f_t = 2u_t - \bar{u}_t$$

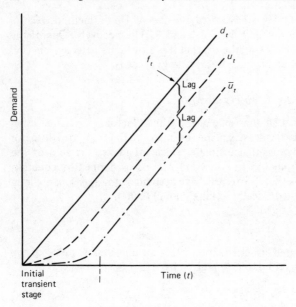

Fig. 2.5 Illustration of the lagged response of an exponentially weighted average to a linear additive trend

However, under steady state conditions the actual and estimated lags can be equated so that

$$u_t - \bar{u}_t = \frac{1 - \alpha}{\alpha} b_t$$

where λ is now replaced by its estimate b_t and hence

$$b_t = \frac{\alpha}{1 - \alpha} (u_t - \bar{u}_t) \qquad (2.8)$$

Thus the forecast for d_t at any time τ is given by

$$f_{t+T} = f_t + b_t \tau \qquad (2.9)$$

or

$$f_{t+\tau} = 2u_t - \bar{u}_t + \frac{\alpha}{1 - \alpha} (u_t - \bar{u}_t)\tau \qquad (2.10)$$

which simplifies, for the one-period-ahead forecast (i.e. $\tau = 1$), to

$$f_{t+1} = \frac{(2 - \alpha)u_t - \bar{u}_t}{1 - \alpha} \qquad (2.11)$$

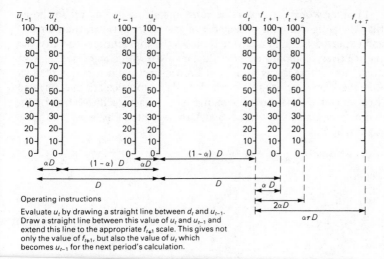

Fig. 2.6 Generalized Nomogram to evaluate the τ-periods ahead forecast in linear additive trend situations (Brown's double smoothed model)

The advantage of this method of Brown's is that is is a single parameter system and can also be evaluated using a 'two-move' Nomogram (see Fig. 2.6).

(iv) Brown's adaptive smoothing method

Brown's[3] second method assumes that, given a sales or demand sequence which is known or assumed to have some underlying model, the most logical approach is to perform a regression analysis (which minimizes the sum of squared errors) on the data and also to make it a *weighted* regression, by giving more attention to recent data. It would appear reasonable to assume in this situation that the importance of an observation for prediction purposes diminishes by a given percentage each month. Thus, if locally, at time t the sales or demand at a time $t + \tau$ are given by the underlying model as

$$d_{t+\tau} = a_0 + a_1\tau + a_2\tau^2 + \epsilon_t \qquad (2.12)$$

where ϵ_t is a random error with zero mean, then, given γ (which corresponds to the monthly discount of an observation) at time t, we should choose a_0, a_1 and a_2 so that

$$\sum_{i=0}^{\infty} \gamma^i (d_{t-i} - f_{t-i})^2 \text{ is a minimum.}$$

In other words, at time t the constants a_0, a_1 and a_2 are so chosen that the weighted sum of squares of the errors between the observed and expected is a minimum. It is obviously impracticable to carry out the relatively complicated procedure involved with a regression analysis every time a forecast is made, but Brown's method is based on the fact that there is a very simple method available to calculate the weighted least-squares estimate of d_t, unique to the linear additive trend case.

For a linear additive trend model, the weighted least-square estimate is given by

$$f_{t+\tau} = u_t + b_t \tau \tag{2.13}$$

where

$$u_t = u_{t-1} + b_{t-1} + (1 - \gamma^2)e_t \tag{2.14}$$

$$e_t = d_t - f_t \tag{2.15}$$

and

$$b_t = b_{t-1} + (1 - \gamma)^2 e_t \tag{2.16}$$

This weighted regression method has several attractive features. These are:

(a) A logical, clear and easily understood concept, i.e. minimizing the weighted sum of squares of the forecasting error.

(b) It is a one-parameter method in which γ represents the period discount factor (i.e. it is equivalent to $(1 - \alpha)$ in other methods).

(c) The coefficients of the forecasting model are jointly estimated, thus reducing auto correlation.

(d) It is simple to operate, given that it will be used within a computerized forecasting system.

This method would appear to have replaced Holt's method at I.C.I. (ref. Harrison[4]) and a value of $\gamma = 0.8$ is recommended. A flow diagram indicating the computer logic for this model is given as Appendix B.

(v) Box–Jenkins method

The original Box–Jenkins[1] approach to forecasting was through control theory and was, therefore, not developed with demand forecasting specifically in mind. The general statement of the Box–Jenkins three-term predictor is

$$u_t = u_{t-1} + \gamma_{-1}(e_t - e_{t-1}) + \gamma_0 e_t + \gamma_1 \sum_{t=0}^{-\infty} e_t \tag{2.17}$$

where e_t is defined as in equation (2.15).

For those readers acquainted with servomechanism control theory, the term with the γ_0 coefficient is the 'proportioned' control term, that with γ_1 the 'integral' control term, and that with γ_{-1} the 'derivative' control term. Box and Jenkins in their original paper did not recommend the use of the derivative (or error difference) term for demand forecasting and other writers have supported this view. In spite of this and the fact that three parameters have to be specified, the 'Box–Jenkins three-term predictor' has been utilized by some computer systems.

Ward[9], using 'z' transform techniques, has shown that Holt's, Brown's double exponential smoothing, and the Box–Jenkins methods are all particular cases of a more general model and that the three will be exactly the same if the parameter values of A, B, γ_1, $\gamma-1$ and γ_0 are related to α as follows:

$$A = \gamma_0 = \alpha(2 - \alpha) \tag{2.18}$$

$$B = \frac{\alpha}{2 - \alpha} \tag{2.19}$$

$$\gamma_1 = \alpha^2 \tag{2.20}$$

and equivalent values over the range of interest are given in Table 2.1.

TABLE 2.1. Equivalence of parameters

α	0.050	0.100	0.200	0.300
$A = \gamma_0$	0.098	0.190	0.350	0.510
B	0.026	0.052	0.111	0.176
γ_1	0.0025	0.010	0.040	0.090
γ_{-1}	0.0000	0.000	0.000	0.000

Thus it would appear that these three methods are all basically the same. For the one-period-ahead forecast Brown's double smoothing method is also exactly the same as Muir's adaptation of Holt's method. Holt's method does allow one to over- or underestimate the trend if required (by altering B) and the Box–Jenkin's method permits values of γ_0, γ_1 and γ_{-1} which are greater than one or negative, and there are situations where such values could be needed. However, Brown's adaptive smoothing method, with its underlying concept of discounted weighted regression, is a radically different method from the others so far described and appears generally to produce less forecasting errors (see Table 2.2). In the author's experience this model also appears to have the facility to 'lock-on' to a trend once it has recognized it. Because two squaring functions are involved it is recommended that this method be used only for a computerized forecasting system.

TABLE 2.2. Table of standard deviations of forecasting errors over initial 50 periods

Demand	$A = 0.1$ $B = 0.01$ Holt	$\alpha = 0.1$ Brown (D)	$\gamma_0 = 0.2$ $\gamma_1 = 0.1$ Box-Jenkins	$\alpha = 0.3$ Brown (A)
Ramp $d_t = N$	1.483	1.583	1.209	0.284
Step $d_t = 50$	12.503	9.822	12.359	8.095
Impulse $d_t = 50$ at $t = 10$	7.310	7.617	7.633	12.380*
Exponential $d_t = \exp(\tau/10)$	15.721	11.200	10.909	0.751

*The reason for the poor showing of Brown's (A) method in response to an impulse function is that, being essentially an error-actuated predictor, it cannot predict an impulse until after it has occurred. However, afterwards, this method resettles to the pre-impulse level far quicker than the others.

(aB) Linear ratio trend forecasting models

(i) Muir's[7] method

If it is suspected that, instead of changes in the process average μ (as incorporated in equation (2.0)) varying linearly with time as in the previous model, changes in μ are likely to be proportional to μ itself (i.e. linear on a logarithmic scale) then a ratio model may be more appropriate.

This can be written as

$$d_t = (d_{t-1} - \epsilon_{t-1})\rho + \epsilon_t \qquad (2.21)$$

where ρ is a ratio trend factor.

It is not possible to use the same smoothing function u_t as for the additive case and, hence, a new function v_t is introduced, where

$$v_t = d_t + (1 - \alpha)r_t\, v_{t-1} \qquad (2.22)$$

where r, an unbiased estimate of ρ (the ratio trend factor of the process generating d_t) is given initially by:

$$r_t = \alpha d_t/v_{t-1} + (1 - \alpha)r_{t-1} \qquad (2.23)$$

Then forecasts for the period $t + \tau$ are given by

$$f_{t+\tau} = v_t\, r_t^{\tau} \qquad (2.24)$$

Ratio trend methods of forecasting do not appear to be popular although Muir shows that, on certain types of demand data, improved forecasts are made with a ratio rather than linear trend model. Linear trend models can however be converted into ratio models by taking logarithmic transformations of the observations.

(cA) Combined linear and seasonal additive trend models

Seasonality is usually dealt with by using a decomposition forecasting method, which assumes that the underlying influences generating data values such as stationarity, linearity and seasonality can be separately identified and their values estimated. The forecasting process is then a matter of 'recomposing' the separated elements to produce the forecast.

Because in seasonal situations it is necessary to identify how the data value in each time period (i.e. month) compares with those in other time periods within the seasonal cycle (usually a year) and since each particular time period only occurs once per cycle; to establish the 'shape' of the seasonal pattern a minimum of four years of data is usually required. Such seasonal patterns are described numerically by de-seasonalizing factors, which represent the ratio of the expected value in a particular time period within the seasonal cycle compared with the current average value for all time periods within that cycle. Thus for a product with increased retail sales prior to Christmas and also during the summer months, the following pattern of L de-seasonalizing factors might be established (Table 2.3). Where L is the number of time periods within the seasonal cycle ($L = 12$ for calendar months, 4 for quarters and sometimes 13 for those companies working to a thirteen accounting period year).

TABLE 2.3. Monthly de-seasonalizing factors (established from at least four years of data)

1980												1981	
Jan.	Feb.	Mar.	Apr.	May	June	July	Aug.	Sept.	Oct.	Nov.	Dec.	Jan.	Feb.
0.8	0.7	0.8	0.9	1.1	1.2	1.3	1.2	1.1	1.0	0.9	1.2		

For seasonal forecasting it is always necessary to store the last L de-seasonalizing factors and because of this, some systems group products thought to be influenced similarly by seasonal effects under the same set of de-seasonalizing factors. This both reduces data storage costs and can also produce a more stable and representative set of factors.

It should be noted that the sum of the de-seasonalizing factors in Table 2.3 comes to twelve (i.e. an average of one) and this is a necessary requirement if unbiased forecasts are to be produced. Most decomposition models assume that some form of linear trend may exist and therefore, incorporate an equation to estimate the value of that trend. This is because if the data being analysed were to be subject to such a linear trend which was not separately estimated, the de-seasonalizing factors would very rapidly become biased, i.e. depart from a sum of twelve.

(i) The Holt–Winter de-seasonalized forecasting model[5, 10]

The Holt–Winter model is a decomposition model incorporating exponentially weighted averages. Estimates of the underlying stationary linear and seasonal elements are evaluated as follows:

(a) Stationary element (i.e. average monthly value — irrespective of the season). The equation for estimating the stationary element (equation (2.25)) is the same as Holt's original proposal (equation (2.1)) with the exception that the current raw data value d_t is de-seasonalized by dividing it by F_{t-L}, the de-seasonalizing factor of L periods ago, which is the most recent estimate of the de-seasonalizing factor for the month in question. Thus (referring to Table 2.3) if the raw value of d_t in January 1981 was 1600 units, the de-seasonalized value would be $1600/0.8 = 2000$ units.

$$u_t = A\frac{d_t}{F_{t-L}} + (1 - A)(u_{t-1} + b_{t-1}) \qquad (2.25)$$

(b) Linear element — evaluated as in Holt's growth model using:

$$b_t = B(u_t - u_{t-1}) + (1 - B)b_{t-1} \qquad (2.26)$$

(c) Seasonal element (i.e. updating of the de-seasonalizing factors). Because the de-seasonalizing factors represents the ratio of the raw data value to the overall or stationary average, in any period the current estimate of that ratio is d_t/u_t. Thus the exponentially weighted average estimate of the current de-seasonalizing factor F_t is define as:

$$F_t = C\frac{d_t}{u_t} + (1 - C)F_{t-L} \qquad (2.27)$$

(d) Forecast. Having individually estimated the three underlying elements, the forecast for the τ periods ahead $(f_{t+\tau})$ is evaluated by 'recomposing' those elements such that the growth element is added to the stationary element u_t and the result 'seasonalized' by multiplying by the appropriate de-seasonalizing factor $F_{t-L+\tau}$. Thus:

$$f_{t+\tau} = (u_t + b_t\,\tau)F_{t-L+\tau} \qquad (2.28)$$

To assist readers in understanding this more complex model, let us assume that in the seasonal situation described in Table 2.3 that past average monthly sales (u_{t-1}) were 2000 units and that a no-growth situation exited $(b_{t-1} = 0)$. Therefore, given no random error and a perfectly behaved model, the expected sales in January 1981 would be 1600 units. Assuming that such an idyllic situation did not exist, let us assume that sales in January were actually 1750 units and then examine how the Holt–Winter model attempts to explain the unexpected additional sales of 150 units. With $A = 0.2, B = 0.2$ and

$C = 0.5$ (of which, more later) the reader can confirm for himself by using equations (2.25) through (2.27) that updated values for u_t, b_t and F_t become 2037.5 units, 7.5 units and 0.83 respectively.

The interpretation of these results is that the average monthly (i.e. de-seasonalized) sales have increased in a step of 37.5 units from 2000 to 2037.5 units, that growth per month has increased from zero to 7.5 units and that January's de-seasonalizing factor has been increased from 0.8 to 0.83. All these changes are the model's attempted explanation of the 150 additional units of sales in January 1981.

Using these new, updated values in equation (2.27) the forecast for sales in February 1981 would be 1431.5 units rather than 1400 units which would have been the forecast had the additional 150 units not occurred in January.

Because of the relative complexity of the Holt—Winter model, it is invariably only used when a computer is available. Where the reader does not have access to a standard forecasting package which includes the Holt—Winter model, Appendix C offers a flow-diagram indicating the associated logic and calculations involved.

Thamara[8] has shown that improved forecasts for the seasonal additive type of demand situation may be made by ensuring that the average of all the de-seasonalizing factors can be made unity for the year preceding the year in which forecasts are to be made. This can be arranged by making

$$\sum_{L=0}^{11} \frac{F_{t-L}}{12} = 1$$

These improved forecasts follow because theoretically, and in practice, the de-seasonalizing factors calculated by the standard exponential smoothing model could have an average that deviates from one. In effect, this then would bias predictions up or down depending on whether the average of the factors was greater or less than one. Thamara also found that in a large number of demand situations, values of A, B and C of 0.2, 0.2 and 0.5 respectively turned out to be the best weighting factors for such demand situations, a higher weight being given to the de-seasonalizing element because of its infrequent updating. Winter[10] in an earlier study had also found that similar values, namely 0.2, 0.2 and 0.6 for A, B and C respectively, produced a minimum standard deviation of forecasting errors.

In practice the Holt—Winter model is the most used forecasting model for seasonal data. Its forecasting accuracy compares very favourably with much more expensive and sophisticated models when the data being analysed are relatively well behaved (i.e. the mean absolute percentage error, see page 40, is less than 50 per cent). For data less well behaved than this, the model has difficulty identifying the separate, underlying components.

(ii) Brown's generalized adaptive smoothing method

This method is the same weighted least-squares estimate already described (page 27) but now using more sophisticated models on which the weighted regressions are based. This technique tends to be rather complicated and involved: those readers interested further should refer to Brown[3]. Harrison[4] has shown that, when applying Brown's adaptive smoothing to seasonal models, the value of γ (the regression's discount factor) requires to be large enough to provide a reasonable amount of weight to at least ten data points, but small enough to validate the assumption that the model holds locally. This conflicting requirement on γ can often invalidate Brown's model when applied to a seasonal situation, but does not occur in the linear form.

(cB) Combined linear and seasonal ratio trend model

In this model it is assumed that the process generating the data values is subjected to a linear, ratio trend.

Using a similar argument as for the additive model, the exponentially smoothed average for the ratio trend situation is calculated using

$$u_t = \frac{Ad_t}{F_{t-L}} + (1 - A)(1 + b_{t-1})u_{t-1} \qquad (2.29)$$

and the linear trend factor is calculated using

$$b_t = B\frac{u_t - u_{t-1}}{u_{t-1}} + (1 - B)b_{t-1} \qquad (2.30)$$

F_t is calculated on the same basis as before, using equation (2.26), and the resulting forecasting for the linear and seasonal ratio trend model is given by

$$f_{t+\tau} = u_t(1 + b_t)^\tau F_{t-L+\tau}. \qquad (2.31)$$

Summary of most applicable forecasting methods used in non-stationary demand situations

(aA) Linear additive trends

There have been more forecasting models proposed for this type of trend than any other so, rather than summarize details of all the methods proposed earlier in the chapter, the best two for either manual or computer implementation will be briefly described.

Manual method

Because of its single parameter and ease of calculation, Brown's would appear to be the best for a manually operated forecasting system being used in a linear additive trend demand situation since forecasts can be evaluated using a simple two-move Nomogram (Fig. 2.6).

Computer method (for flow diagram see Appendix B)

Because of its simple concept of weighted regression but rather complicated calculations, Brown's adaptive smoothing method would appear most suitable for computer implementation, where the complexity of calculation is not a restraining factor.

Here the stationary element is given by

$$u_t = u_{t-1} + b_{t-1} + (1 - \gamma^2)e_t$$

where

$$e_t = d_t - f_t$$

The growth factor is calculated as

$$b_t = b_{t-1} + (1 - \gamma)^2 e_t$$

and the forecast for the period τ periods ahead is again given by

$$f_{t+\tau} = u_t + b_t \tau$$

where it is recommended that $\gamma = 0.8$.

(aB) Linear ratio trend

Muir's method is the most used of those documented for use in this situation. For this method the permanent component is given by

$$V_t = d_t + (1 - \alpha)r_t \, V_{t-1}$$

where the ratio trend factor is given initially by

$$r_t = \alpha d_t / V_{t-1} + (1 - \alpha)r_{t-1}$$

and the forecast for the period τ periods ahead is given by

$$f_{t+\tau} = V_t \, r_t^{\tau}$$

(cA) Combined linear and seasonal additive trend model (Appendix C)

The additive model appears to be used far more than the ratio model in this situation. The Holt-Winter model is defined as follows.

Permanent component is given by

$$u_t = A \frac{d_t}{F_{t-L}} + (1 - A)(u_{t-1} + b_{t-1})$$

The de-seasonalizing factor is calculated as

$$F_t = \frac{C d_t}{u_t} + (1 - C)F_{t-L}$$

where there are L time periods in the seasonal cycle.

The linear trend factor is then calculated, as in the linear case, as

$$b_t = B(u_t - u_{t-1}) + (1 - B)b_{t-1}$$

and the forecast for the period $t + \tau$ is given by

$$f_{t+\tau} = (u_t + b_t T)F_{t-L+\tau}$$

where $F_{t-L+\tau}$ is the last calculated de-seasonalizing factor corresponding to the period $t + \tau$. Recommended values for A, B and C are 0.2, 0.2 and 0.6 respectively.

References

1 BOX, G.E.P. AND JENKINS, C.M. (1962) 'Some statistical aspects of adaptive optimization and control', *Journal of the Royal Statistical Society* (B), **24**, 297

2 BROWN, R.G. (1959) *Statistical Forecasting for Inventory Control*, New York, McGraw-Hill

3 BROWN, R.G. (1962) *Smoothing, Forecasting and Prediction of Discrete Time Series*, New Jersey, Prentice-Hall

4 HARRISON, P.J. (1964) 'Short-term sales forecasting', *Applied Statistics*, Series C, **14**, 102

5 HOLT, C.C. (1957) *Forecasting Seasonals by Exponentially Weighted Moving Averages*, Office of Naval Research Memo. No. 52

6 I.C.I. (1964) *Short-term Forecasting*, I.C.I. monograph No. 2, Edinburgh, Oliver & Boyd

7 MUIR, A. (1958) 'Automatic sales forecasting', *Computer Journal*, **1**, 113

8 THAMARA, T. (1968) *Exponential Smoothing with Automatic Weight Assignment*, paper presented at the TIMS/ORSA Joint National Meeting San Francisco

9 WARD, D.H. (1963) 'Comparison of different systems of exponentially weighted prediction', *Statistician*, **13**, No. 3, 173

10 WINTER, P.R. (1960) 'Forecasting sales by exponentially weighted moving averages', *Management Science*, **6**, 324

Chapter 3

Measuring the dispersion of forecasting errors

The standard deviation

As mentioned in Chapter 1, page 9, the usual measure of spread or dispersion of a variable about its average value is the standard deviation. The standard deviation is defined as the square-root of the 'variance' which is itself defined as the 'average of the sum of *squared* errors'.

The principal reason that the measure of dispersion is made dependent on the sum of squared errors, rather than just the sum of errors, is that, by squaring, all errors (whether positive or negative) contribute to the measure of spread. In most forecasting situations the sum of errors would, in fact, tend toward zero as the effect of positive and negative errors cancel each other out. Such a measure would, therefore, give no indication whatever of the degree of spread.

There are of course other good reasons for using the standard deviation as a measure of spread, and these depend mainly on its mathematical properties, which are made use of primarily in tests of statistical significance.

Unfortunately the orthodox statistical calculations involved in determining the value of the variance, and hence the standard deviation, are too complicated and tedious to be applied in the forecasting situation. An alternative method is, therefore, more generally used to estimate the standard deviation.

Instead of squaring all errors to ensure that, whether positive or negative in value, all contribute to a measure of spread, another approach could be based on the assumption that all errors were considered to be positive irrespective of whether they were originally positive or negative. This is known as taking the *absolute values* or *modulus* of the errors, and provides a very simple procedure for estimating the standard deviation.

The forecasting error e_t has already been defined as the difference between the actual demand d_t and the forecast f_t, such that

$$e_t = d_t - f_t \tag{3.1}$$

Now instead of calculating the variance as the sum of squared errors,

37

we can define another measure of spread known as the *mean absolute deviation* of errors (MAD_t). As its name indicates, the mean absolute deviation is simply the mean or average of the absolute values of errors or deviations. In Chapter 1 it was shown that the exponentially weighted average was a true form of average; so there is no reason why the mean absolute deviation cannot be calculated as the exponentially weighted average of the absolute value of errors, as given by

$$MAD_t = \alpha|e_t| + (1 - \alpha)MAD_{t-1} \tag{3.2}$$

Where the two straight lines either side of e_t indicate that $|e_t|$ is regarded as positive in this calculation, even should the true value of e_t be negative (i.e. if f_t is greater than d_t).

Having calculated the mean absolute deviation (MAD_t), it is now necessary to show how this can be used to estimate the standard deviation (σ_t). It so happens that for a wide range of statistical distributions the standard deviation is slightly larger than the mean absolute deviation, but directly proportional to it. The constant of proportionality varies slightly between distributions but generally the value is between 1.2 and 1.3*, so a value of 1.25 is usually adopted as a compromise: hence

$$\sigma_t = 1.25 \, MAD_t \tag{3.3}$$

Thus the procedure required to estimate the standard deviation of forecasting errors is:

(i) Calculate the forecasting error as the difference between the actual demand and the forecast (equation (3.1)).

(ii) Calculate the new value of the mean absolute deviation MAD_t (equation (3.2)).

(iii) Multiply the new value of the mean absolute deviation by 1.25 to obtain the new estimate of the standard deviation (equation (3.3)).

This complete procedure is illustrated in Table 3.1, which uses exactly the same demand data as for the forecasting exercise represented in Chapter 1, Table 1.3. The analysis shows that the value of the standard deviation of the monthly demand series of values is 14 units approximately.

The main reason for calculating the standard deviation is that it is a basic measure of forecasting accuracy*. For relatively short forecasting horizons, it can be assumed, with a very high degree of confidence, that future data values will fall within an envelope of plus or minus two standard deviations either side of the forecast. Thus in Table 3.1, we

*For the Normal distribution the value is $\sqrt{\pi/2} = 1.2533$

*The standard deviation is also used in inventory control packages in evaluating safety stocks.

TABLE 3.1. Typical forecasting schedule including calculation of the standard deviation ($\alpha = 0.2$)

		Jan.	Feb.	Mar.	Apr.	May	June	July	Aug.	Sep.	Oct.	Nov.	Dec.	Jan.
This month's demand	d_t	60	70	55	80	90	65	70	75	60	80	90	100	95
Last month's forecast for this month	u_{t-1}	70	68	68	65	68	72	71	71	72	70	72	76	81
$\alpha \times$ this month's demand	αd_t	12.0	14.0	11.0	16.0	18.0	13.0	14.0	15.0	12.0	16.0	18.0	20.0	19.0
$(1-\alpha) \times$ last month's forecast for this month	$(1-\alpha)u_{t-1}$	56.0	54.4	54.4	52.0	54.4	57.6	56.8	56.8	57.6	56.0	57.6	60.8	64.8
This month's forecast for next month (rounded)	$u_t = \alpha d_t + (1-\alpha)u_{t-1}$	68	68	65	68	72	71	71	72	70	72	76	81	84
This month's forecasting error	$e_t = d_t - f_t$	-10	2	-13	15	22	-7	-1	4	-12	10	18	24	14
$\alpha \times$ this month's forecasting error's absolute value	$\alpha\lvert e_t\rvert$	2.0	0.4	2.6	3.0	4.4	1.4	0.2	0.8	2.4	2.0	3.6	4.8	2.8
$(1-\alpha) \times$ last month's mean absolute deviation	$(1-\alpha)\text{MAD}_{t-1}$	5.6*	6.1	5.2	6.2	7.4	9.4	8.6	7.0	6.2	6.9	7.1	8.6	10.7
This month's mean absolute deviation	$\text{MAD}_t = \alpha\lvert e_t\rvert + (1-\alpha)\text{MAD}_{t-1}$	7.6	6.5	7.8	9.2	11.8	10.8	8.8	7.8	8.6	8.9	10.7	13.4	13.5
This month's standard deviation	$1.25\,\text{MAD}_t$	9.5	8.1	9.8	11.5	14.8	13.5	11.0	9.8	10.8	11.1	13.4	16.8	16.9

*Estimate based on initial $\text{MAD}_{t-1} = \frac{1}{10}u_{t-1}$ which is generally suitable for industrial and business data

could confidently expect the data value in February (following the final January) to fall within an envelope of $(84 \pm 2 \times 16.9)$ units, i.e. from approximately 50 to 118 units.

It cannot be stressed too strongly that forecasts should always be accompanied by the standard deviation. A sales forecast of 1000 units and an associated standard deviation of 100 units means that expected sales should fall within an envelope of 800 units to 1200 units which is reasonably meaningful. However, the same forecast of a 1000 units and a standard deviation of 400 units is virtually meaningless and could be replaced by the statement 'We might sell some next month!'

The mean absolute percentage error

The mean absolute percentage error (MAPE), as the name suggests, is the mean or average value of the absolute forecasting errors as a percentage of the respective data value. As such it can be defined as:

$$\text{MAPE} = \frac{1}{n} \sum_{t=0}^{n-1} \frac{|e_t|}{d_t} \times 100 \qquad (3.4)$$

For the forecasting errors and data in Table 3.1 the MAPE can be evaluated as 15 per cent.

The MAPE is a most useful measure in comparing the accuracy of forecasts between different items or products since it measures *relative* performance. Typical MAPE values for industrial and business data and their interpretation are shown in Table 3.2.

TABLE 3.2. Interpretation of typical MAPE values

MAPE (%)	Interpretation
< 10	Highly accurate forecasting
10–20	Good forecasting
20–50	Reasonable forecasting
> 50	Inaccurate forecasting

Note that if $d_t = 0$ in equation (3.4) the result is theoretically infinity. Many commercial forecasting packages which evaluate the MAPE cannot accept zero data values because of this. More robust packages (see Appendix D) bypass this calculation when $d_t = 0$ and also reduce the count n by one.)

Mean percentage error and mean error

The mean percentage error (MPE) and mean error (ME) are both measures of forecasting *bias*. Based on the general assumption that costs of over-prediction are the same as costs of under-prediction in industrial and business forecasting ideally forecasts should be unbiased and, hence, both of these measures should ideally approach zero. In practice both measures of bias should be small. Being a relative measure, the MPE defined as:

$$\text{MPE} = \frac{1}{n} \sum_{t=0}^{n-1} \frac{e_t}{d_t} \times 100 \tag{3.5}$$

is the more useful and should generally be less than 5 per cent, and as with MAPE, does not like zero values.

The mean error, although not a relative measure, does give an indication in units as to how much the forecast is biased and is defined as:

$$\text{ME} = \frac{1}{n} \sum_{t=0}^{n-1} e_t \tag{3.6}$$

For the forecasting errors and data in Table 3.1 the MPE and ME are 3.86 per cent and 5 units respectively. The reason for these relatively high values is the increase in demand values from October onwards for which the simple exponentially weighted average forecast really is not appropriate (see Chapter 2).

The mean squared error or sum of squared errors

The mean squared error (MSE) defined as:

$$\text{MSE} = \frac{1}{n} \sum_{t=0}^{n-1} e_t^2 \tag{3.7}$$

or the equivalent sum of squared errors (SSE) defined as:

$$\text{SSE} = \sum_{t=0}^{n-1} e_t^2 \tag{3.8}$$

is the measure most used when optimal forecasting models are being sought. Many commercial forecasting packages use the minimizing of the MSE or SSE as their criterion for selecting model parameters, such as the values of α in simple exponential smoothing, where users ask for this facility rather than specifying the parameter(s) themselves.

Appendix D is a flow diagram, which indicates the necessary logic and calculations required to evaluate all the measures of dispersion of forecasting errors discussed in this chapter.

Exercise

For the data presented in Table 3.1 show that the values of the MAPE, MPE and ME are respectively 15.01 per cent, 3.86 per cent and 5.08.

Chapter 4

Monitoring short-term forecasting systems (the smoothed error method)

Once any routine system for making forecasts has been set up, it is essential to have some form of monitoring method to indicate when demand becomes so different from that expected, that the forecasting system effectively breaks down. All forecasts are delayed in their response to sudden changes, and the resultant lags brought about by such delays naturally produce larger than usual forecasting errors. For

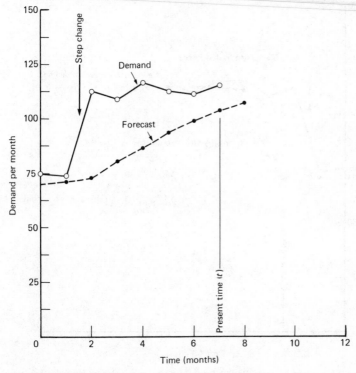

Fig. 4.1 Typical response of an exponentially weighted average forecast to a step change in demand ($\alpha = 0.2$)

example, a typical exponentially weighted average forecast's response to a step change in demand can be seen in Fig. 4.1. Here, for several periods after the change has occurred, the forecast is far too low, hence producing large forecasting errors.

Thus a major reason for monitoring a short-term forecasting system is to ensure that sudden demand changes are highlighted, so that the reasons for any such changes can be investigated. Once a monitoring method has indicated the forecast's lack of control, as illustrated in Fig. 4.1, questions can be asked as to what is responsible for this sudden change, and whether the change is likely to be sustained or not and, if not, when is it likely to end. Such information obviously cannot be derived from the forecasting system itself, and it is in this type of situation that the market intelligence of the company's salesforce must be resorted to, however subjective or biased that may be.

Suppose the company's salesforce, on investigation of the situation indicated in Fig. 4.1, found that the increase in demand was likely to

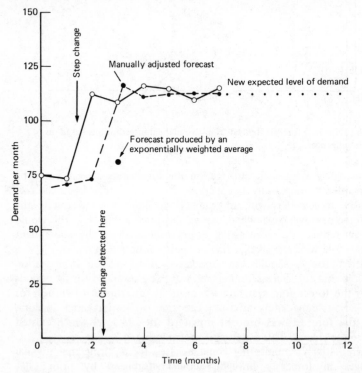

Fig. 4.2 Improved forecast derived from manual interruption based on sales intelligence

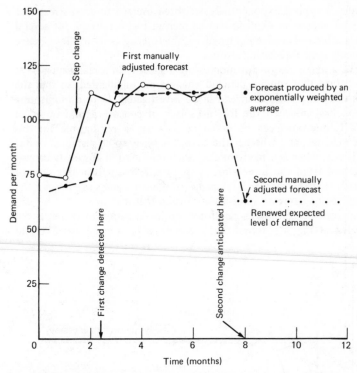

Fig. 4.3 Improved forecast derived from two manual interruptions based on sales intelligence

be sustained. With such information the forecasting system could be interrupted perhaps only two periods after the change had occurred, and the forecast brought up manually to some value nearer to the expected new average-demand level as illustrated in Fig. 4.2. This would greatly reduce the forecasting errors generated in the subsequent periods following the change, had no special action been taken.

Alternatively, should the company's salesforce on investigation indicate that the increase in demand was to be sustained for six periods only, the forecasting system could again be interrupted to ensure, for the period immediately after the cessation of the increased demand, that the forecast was brought down to the old level which existed before the change. This situation is shown in Fig. 4.3.

Alternatively, monitoring could be used for ensuring that manual changes in forecasts brought about beforehand by prior sales intelligence are matched by the predicted increase in demand. For instance, if sales intelligence indicates a future step increase in demand

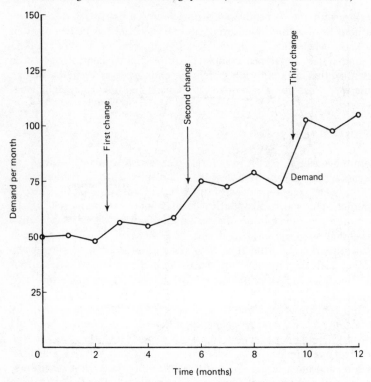

Fig. 4.4 Series of demand changes which may or may not be statistically significant

and forecasts are altered to meet this, if the increase fails to occur the monitoring system will indicate this feature. Only if the step increase in demand occurs as predicted will the monitoring system not respond. Reasons causing such situations could be the introduction or dropping of a product, a design modification, or even planned exceptional promotional activity; all of which are often known months in advance.

From the foregoing discussion it is fairly evident that there is a definite need for monitoring forecasting systems. To some extent the graphical illustrations have not emphasized this point far enough, as the fact that a change in demand has occurred in Figs 4.1–3 is readily apparent by visual inspection. However, in practice it is obviously impossible to plot a graph of every demand value for all stocked items and, even if it were possible, who — by visual inspection — could say of the examples shown in Fig. 4.4 which were significant changes and which were not?

The same is also true of a manual listing method; although the clerk dealing with the demand figures might sense a rise or fall in demand, without a formalized monitoring system he would not be in a position to know when such a rise or fall was significant or not. For a forecasting system developed completely for computer control, again it is essential that a monitoring system be employed, as even the human observers' 'feel' for a rise or fall in demand has now been eliminated.

Statistical significance

Before describing specific monitoring methods, it would be advisable to discuss what is meant by a *significant* demand change. In mathematical terms, when the term significant is used 'statistical significance' is inferred. The statistical significance of whether an event is likely to occur or not depends on the statistical distribution of that event's likelihood of occurrence, and this may be difficult to determine in many situations. Fortunately, here we are not concerned with determining such distributions but simply with interpreting the results of such analyses and, in particular, what the term 'statistically significant' means.

If a statistician says that he is 95 per cent confident (i.e. statistically confident) of an event happening he means that, on average, he would expect the event to occur 95 times out of 100. Five times out of 100, however, he would expect the event not to occur, purely for random reasons and not because the system controlling the event's occurrence had in any way changed. Thus, with a variable situation the statistician accepts that he can never be 100 per cent certain of a particular outcome, so he expresses his confidence in terms of a level of confidence. This level is usually chosen between 90 per cent and 95 per cent when dealing with forecasting and stock control situations. Thus if a change is indicated at a '95 per cent confidence level' this change is regarded as 'statistically significant'.

The smoothed error method

Trigg's[3] method of monitoring, proposed in 1964, was an improvement on a method proposed by Brown[2] some two years earlier. As the method is based on the calculation of the exponentially weighted average of the error, it is usually referred to as the 'smoothed error method'.

The smoothed error method proposed by Trigg is based on the definition of a 'tracking signal' whose value indicates, with degrees of statistical confidence, the failure of a forecasting system caused by a change in the demand pattern.

This tracking signal is defined as the ratio of the exponentially smoothed error $(\overline{e}_t)$ to the mean absolute deviation (MAD_t).

As the mean absolute deviation is already required as an estimate of the standard deviation, evaluation of the tracking signal requires only one further calculation, namely that of the smoothed error $\overline{e}_t$, which is given by

$$\overline{e}_t = \alpha e_t + (1 - \alpha)\overline{e}_{t-1} \tag{4.1}$$

This equation is of the same form as that for the mean absolute deviation (equation (3.2)) with the exception that the modulus sign for e_t is omitted and thus the sign of e_t is now taken into account. Having defined $\overline{e}_t$, the tracking signal (T_t) is then defined as

$$T_t = \overline{e}_t / \mathrm{MAD}_t \tag{4.2}$$

Trigg indicates that this tracking signal has a range of ±1 and can be shown to have calculable statistical confidence levels as indicated in Table 4.1. For this method the same smoothing constant (α) would usually be used for calculating the forecast, the mean absolute deviation and the smoothed error, more often than not either 0.1 or 0.2.

TABLE 4.1. Values for the tracking signal

Level of confidence (i.e. cumulative probability) (%)	Trigg's tracking signal (T_t)	
	$\alpha = 0.1$	$\alpha = 0.2$
80	0.36	0.54
90	0.45	0.66
95	0.51	0.74
98	0.60	0.81
100	1.00	1.00

Thus, for a forecasting system based on a value of $\alpha = 0.1$, if the calculated value of the tracking signal became larger than 0.51 this would indicate with 95 per cent confidence that the forecast had gone out of control owing to some definite change in the demand pattern. (Conversely one would also be 5 per cent confident that T_t exceeded 0.51 for purely random reasons and not because there had been a definite change. At this level of confidence, however, such an alternative is ignored.)

The sign of the tracking signal simply indicates whether the forecast is higher than actual demand (i.e. when T_t is negative) or the actual demand is higher than the forecast (i.e. when T_t is positive)*.

*This is always true if the error is defined as $e_t = d_t - u_{t-1}$ which is the convention usually adopted.

Table 4.2 shows a fully expanded forecasting schedule based on the same demand data as considered in Chapters 1 and 3 but now containing all the necessary components of a comprehensive analysis, namely

(i) a forecast of expected demand based on a simple exponentially weighted average.

(ii) an estimate of the standard deviation of demand based on the mean absolute deviation, and

(iii) a method of monitoring based on the evaluation of the smoothed error tracking signal;

these are all based on a value of $\alpha = 0.2$.

Examining successive values of the tracking signal as evaluated in Table 4.2, it can be seen that up to October these values are very small and, therefore, do not signify any fundamental changes in the demand data. However, in November the value rises to 0.44 and in December to 0.64, which is statistically significant at about the 90 per cent level of confidence. This rise in the value which is maintained so that in January the value has risen to 0.72, is significant at about the 94 per cent level which would usually be high enough to indicate that a fundamental change had occurred. The fact that this last value of the tracking signal is positive indicates that the change has been positive, that is, that there has been a significant *increase* in demand over the past few months. Examination of the actual demand information (which for this period is 75, 60, 80, 90, 100 and 95) verifies this.

In his original paper Trigg indicated that the values quoted for the tracking signal (Table 4.1) were not strictly applicable when using forecasting methods based on exponentially weighted averages, owing to the introduction of serial correlation into the errors — meaning that the forecasting error values were related to each other to some degree, rather than being completely independent. Although indicating this possible degree of inaccuracy in the published values, Trigg did not consider that, in practice, any modifications to these values would be necessary. However, in a later paper Batty[1] has published new and more extensive (in terms of α) values derived from simulation experiments using exponentially weighted averages as forecasts. These figures do differ quite substantially from those originally published and are therefore given here as Table 4.3*.

---

*It has been suggested[2] that the 95% and 99% values can be evaluated as $1.1\sqrt{\alpha}$ and $1.65\sqrt{\alpha}$ respectively, but such values are only valid up to a value of α of 0.3.

TABLE 4.2. Fully expanded forecasting schedule ($\alpha = 0.2$)

		Jan.	Feb.	Mar.
This month's demand	d_t	60	70	55
Last month's forecast for this month	u_{t-1}	70	68	68
$\alpha \times$ this month's demand	αd_t	12.0	14.0	11.0
$(1-\alpha) \times$ last month's forecast for this month	$(1-\alpha)u_{t-1}$	56.0	54.4	54.4
This month's forecast for next month (rounded)	$u_t = \alpha d_t + (1-\alpha)u_{t-1}$	68	68	65
This month's forecasting error	$e_t = d_t - u_{t-1}$	−10	2	−13
$\alpha \times$ this month's forecasting error	αe_t	−2.0	0.4	−2.6
$(1-\alpha) \times$ last month's smoothed error	$(1-\alpha)\bar{e}_{t-1}$	0*	−1.6	−1.0
This month's smoothed error	$\bar{e}_t = \alpha e_t + (1-\alpha)\bar{e}_{t-1}$	−2.0	−1.2	−3.6
$\alpha \times$ the modulus of this month's forecasting error	$\alpha \|e_t\|$	2.0	0.4	2.6
$(1-\alpha) \times$ last month's mean absolute deviation	$(1-\alpha)MAD_{t-1}$	5.6†	6.1	5.2
This month's mean absolute deviation	$MAD_t = \alpha \|e_t\| + (1-\alpha)MAD_{t-1}$	7.6	6.5	7.8
This month's estimate of standard deviation	$\sigma_t = 1.25\, MAD_t$	9.5	8.1	9.8
Tracking signal	$T_t = \bar{e}_t/MAD_t$	−0.26	−0.18	−0.46

*Unbiased initial estimate of $\bar{e}_{t-1} = 0$.

†As before, initial $MAD_{t-1} = \frac{1}{10} u_{t-1}$. It is essential that MAD_{t-1} is initialized, otherwise $T_t = \pm 1$ initially.

Implementing the smoothed error monitoring method

At first sight it might appear that the most effective way of implementing this monitoring method in a forecasting system would be to highlight all items whose values of tracking signal exceeded a blanket value corresponding to a 90 per cent to 95 per cent level of confidence. Indeed, many commercial forecasting packages do just this by highlighting any item whose associated tracking signal value exceeds 0.7. In practice, however, this approach has several disadvantages, namely

(continued)

Apr.	May	June	July	Aug.	Sept.	Oct.	Nov.	Dec.	Jan.
80	90	65	70	75	60	80	90	100	95
65	68	72	71	71	72	70	72	76	81
16.0	18.0	13.0	14.0	15.0	12.0	16.0	18.0	20.0	19.0
52.0	54.4	57.6	56.8	56.8	57.6	56.0	57.6	60.8	64.8
68	72	71	71	72	70	72	76	81	84
15	22	−7	−1	4	−12	10	18	24	14
3.0	4.4	−1.4	−0.2	0.8	−2.4	2.0	3.6	4.8	2.8
−2.9	0.1	3.6	1.8	1.3	1.7	−0.6	1.1	3.8	6.9
0.1	4.5	2.2	1.6	2.1	−0.7	1.4	4.7	8.6	9.7
3.0	4.4	1.4	0.2	0.8	2.4	2.0	3.6	4.8	2.8
6.2	7.4	9.4	8.6	7.0	6.2	6.9	7.1	8.6	10.7
9.2	11.8	10.8	8.8	7.8	8.6	8.9	10.7	13.4	13.5
11.5	14.8	13.5	11.0	9.8	10.8	11.1	13.4	16.8	16.9
0.01	0.38	0.20	0.18	0.27	−0.08	0.16	0.44	0.64	0.72

(i)   A different number of items is highlighted at each review, thus causing an uneven load on the personnel responsible for taking action on highlighted items.

(ii)   The same item can be highlighted month after month, even though it is already known that the forecasting procedure has gone out of control for that item and that remedial action is under way.

(iii) For more expensive items it may be necessary to indicate changes in demand at lower levels of confidence than for cheaper items.

A procedure which resolves these problems and in practice has been found to work well:

(i)   Estimate the maximum number of highlighted items (N) the

TABLE 4.3. Revised values for Trigg's tracking signal

Level of confidence (i.e. cumulative probability) (%)	Tracking signal				
	$\alpha = 0.1$	$\alpha = 0.2$	$\alpha = 0.3$	$\alpha = 0.4$	$\alpha = 0.5$
70	0.24	0.33	0.44	0.53	0.64
80	0.29	0.40	0.52	0.62	0.73
85	0.32	0.45	0.57	0.67	0.77
90	0.35	0.50	0.63	0.72	0.82
95	0.42	0.58	0.71	0.80	0.88
96	0.43	0.60	0.73	0.82	0.89
97	0.45	0.62	0.76	0.84	0.90
98	0.48	0.66	0.79	0.87	0.92
99	0.53	0.71	0.82	0.92	0.94
100	1.00	1.00	1.00	1.00	1.00

'chasing' staff can cope with at each review, and do not allow any more items to be highlighted than this maximum.

(ii) Having selected a level of confidence at which a change in a demand process is felt to be significant for each item, select the top N that exceeds these values.

(Note. It may be necessary to have different levels for different items on some worth or value basis)

(iii) Once an item has been highlighted as being out of control, do not allow it to be included for review for a further three periods, until the remedial action taken is likely to have become effective in getting the forecast back into control.

The approach indicated above simply uses the smoothed error tracking signal as a 'ranking' mechanism and this use of the relative value between items rather than purely individual values negates most arguments as to whether Trigg's or Batty's published values are the more relevant.

In conclusion then, the smoothed error monitoring method is both effective and cheap to operate, its only disadvantage being that it cannot indicate, as the Cusum method can, for how many periods a change in the average data value has been in evidence. (For discussion on Cusums see Chapter 10.)

Appendix A, indicates in flow diagram form, the necessary steps required to calculate the smoothed error tracking signal.

References

1   BATTY, M. (1969) 'Monitoring an exponential smoothing forecasting system', *Operational Research Quarterly*, **20**, 319
2   BROWN, R.G. (1962) *Smoothing, forecasting and prediction of discrete time series*, New Jersey, Prentice-Hall
3   TRIGG, D.W. (1964) 'Monitoring a forecasting system', *Operational Research Quarterly*, **15**, 271

Exercise

Using Table 4.4 with $\alpha = 0.2$, evaluate the smoothed error tracking signal and show that in the final month its value reaches 0.8.

TABLE 4.4. Demand analysis/forecasting worksheet

			55	50	58	49	86	52	54	49	58	68	75	78	82
1	Current demand value	d_t													
2	Forecast	$f_t = u_{t-1}$	50*												
3	Error	$e_t = d_t - u_{t-1}$													
4	Squared error	e_t^2													
5	Cumulative squared error	Σe_t^2													
6	$\alpha \times$ error	αe_t	0.0*												
7	$(1 - \alpha) \times$ past smoothed error	$(1 - \alpha)\,\bar{e}_{t-1}$													
8	Current smoothed error	$\bar{e}_t = \alpha e_t + (1 - \alpha)\bar{e}_{t-1}$													
9	$\alpha \times$ absolute error	$\alpha \lvert e_t \rvert$													
10	$(1 - \alpha) \times$ past MAD	$(1 - \alpha)\mathrm{MAD}_{t-1}$	4.0*												
11	Current MAD	$\mathrm{MAD}_t = \alpha \lvert e_t \rvert + (1-\alpha)\mathrm{MAD}_{t-1}$													
12	Current std dev.	$\sigma_t = 1.25\,\mathrm{MAD}_t$													
13	Tracking signal	$T_t = \bar{e}_t / \mathrm{MAD}_t$													
14	Cumulative error	Σe_t													
15	Exponential weighting constant for forecast	α													
16	$\alpha \times$ current demand	αd_t													
17	$(1 - \alpha) \times$ past forecast	$(1 - \alpha)u_{t-1}$													
18	Next month's forecast	$f_{t+1} = u_t = \alpha\, d_t + (1 - \alpha)u_{t-1}$													

*Estimate or guess

Chapter 5

Adaptive forecasting

Adaptive forecasting is the term used for forecasting methods which 'adapt' themselves to the characteristics of the data or information with which they are dealing. The basic requirement of any such adaptive forecasting method is that, as data become relatively more changeable, the forecast itself responds and becomes more sensitive. Conversely, as the data become relatively more stable the forecast should also become less sensitive.

The need for a forecast to become more sensitive as data become relatively more changeable is fairly evident. A more sensitive forecast will obviously produce smaller lags than a less sensitive one and generally, therefore, will produce better forecasts. The complementary requirement of an insensitive forecast for a stable data situation is not so evident, as in this case both sensitive and insensitive forecasts produce approximately the same forecast values. The need for a very insensitive forecast occurs specifically when a stable data situation is subjected to an occasional single-period impulse, as shown in Fig. 5.1(a). In such a situation, the very insensitive forecast virtually ignores the effect of the impulse and the only large error generated is due to that single, one-off high value. Consider, however, the situation in which the forecasting method is reasonably sensitive and attempts to respond to a single-period impulse as depicted in Fig. 5.1(b). Because all forecasts are delayed in their response by at least one period, any forecast responding to such an impulse will occur one period late, at best. Moreover, one period after the impulse, data values return to normal and thereafter the forecast will also attempt to return to normal, but takes several periods to do so. At each of these periods a forecasting error is generated because the forecasts are still higher than the actual values. Although such errors are of different polarity from that of the error generated in the period of the impulse, all contribute to the sum of squared forecasting errors which, for the sensitive forecast (Fig. 5.1(b)), would essentially be $a^2 + b^2 + c^2 + d^2 + e^2$ as compared with just a^2 for the insensitive forecast (Fig. 5.1(a)).

It is hoped that this naive example has illustrated the general need of all forecasting systems to ignore single-period impulses. Of course such

55

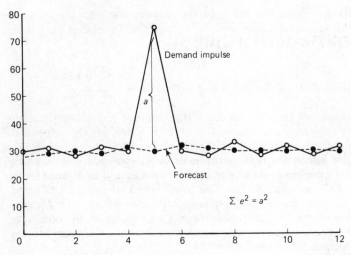

Fig. 5.1(a) Response of an insensitive forecast to a single-period demand impulse

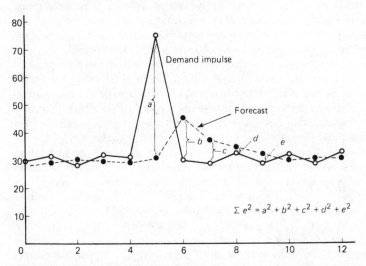

Fig. 5.1(b) Response of a sensitive forecast to a single-period demand impulse

unusually high, instantaneous demand or sales figures still have to be dealt with in practice, but preferably not within a well established forecasting system which is concerned with identifying the underlying data structure, of which single-period impulses are untypical. It is generally preferable to phase such high, single-period values over a longer period of time so that their effects are lessened.

Having established the need for adaptive forecasts, the remainder of this chapter discusses some of the adaptive forecasting models that have been proposed.

Manual method for initiating forecasts

Although not strictly speaking a true adaptive forecasting procedure, many practitioners adopt a very high value of the exponential smoothing constant (α) when initiating forecasts for new products. This ensures that if the initial estimate of sales or demand turns out to be grossly inaccurate, the initial, sensitive forecast will much more rapidly

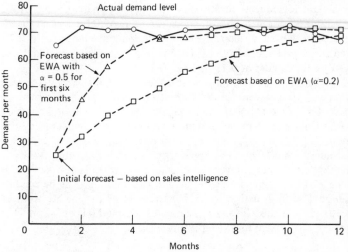

Fig. 5.2 Improved response with increased exponential smoothing constant for first six months

reach the actual demand or sales values than would a forecast based on a more orthodox value of α such as 0.2. This can be readily seen in Fig. 5.2 where α has been set at 0.6 for the first six months and then reduced to 0.2 — a typical scheme operated by many practitioners.

Chow's method[1]

Chow has proposed a method of adaptive forecasting which uses three simultaneous exponentially weighted forecasts based on three different values of α, the exponential smoothing constant.

The actual forecast is based on the 'normal' exponentially weighted average using the central value of α. Either side of the normal exponentially weighted average ('low' and 'high') exponentially weighted averages are generated, based on values of α which are 0.05 lower and higher than the central value. Thus the system could be initiated using forecasts based on $\alpha = 0.1$, with an insensitive or low average based on $\alpha = 0.05$ and a sensitive or high average based on $\alpha = 0.15$.

Having chosen, arbitrarily, the exponential weighting constants for starting, these values are then automatically modified, as time progresses, on the following basis: whenever, on the judgement of an error criterion, one of the 'outer' (high or low) forecasts turns out to be better than the actual (normal) forecast, the next period's forecast is based on the new 'best' forecast. At the same time, new high and low forecasts are introduced surrounding this new normal forecast. Thus, for example, if forecasts based on values of α of 0.05, 0.1 and 0.15 were used initially and, later, the error criterion indicated that the 0.15 proved to be preferable to the 0.1 value, then the system would automatically adopt values of 0.1, 0.15 and 0.2.

Chow has shown that in a practical exercise 59 out of 60 items had, on average, 10 per cent lower forecasting errors using this method instead of a simple exponentially weighted average based on a value of $\alpha = 0.2$. Only one item did not provide improved forecasts using the method.

Although Chow's method appears to provide reasonable results it would appear rather cumbersome compared with Trigg's and with Leach's adaptive response rate method described on page 59 because of the amount of information which has to be stored to generate all three forecasts. It remains, however, an interesting method and represents one of the early attempts at adaptive forecasting.

Thamara's method[4]

Thamara's method is based on the generalized Holt—Winter forecasting model designed to take into account both trend and seasonal factors as well as permanent factors (Chapter 2, page 32).

Thamara arbitrarily assigns differing values to A, the exponential weighting factor of the permanent component of the forecast, in line with the degree of error in the forecasting system. This assignment, as seen in Table 5.1, allows the value of A to vary between 0.2 and 0.5. The upper limit of 0.5 on A was made because, in testing, larger weighting values were found to produce faulty predictions, and

TABLE 5.1. Thamara's assignment of weighting factor with error size

Size of error (%)	Size of exponential weighting factor for stationary element
10	0.20
11	0.22
15	0.30
17	0.34
19	0.38
20	0.40
25 and above	0.50

although this was an empirical conclusion, errors greater than 25 per cent never occurred in practice.

Thamara found that, by applying this method, forecasting errors were reduced when step changes in demand patterns occurred. Judging from tests run with different weights, it appeared that the best weights for the permanent component, trend and seasonal factors were 0.2, 0.2 and 0.5 (corresponding with A, B and C of equations (2.25) to (2.31)) respectively.

Thamara's method appears to be very similar in concept to Chow's except that it is less cumbersome, using only one exponentially weighted average for adaptation.

Trigg and Leach's method[5]

Trigg's proposal (in 1964) for a tracking signal to be used for monitoring purposes in forecasting situations was followed (in 1967) by a proposal, in conjunction with Leach, advocating the use of this same tracking signal in an adaptive response rate forecasting method. In essence, the Trigg and Leach method of adaptive response rate forecasting can be described as follows.

What is principally required of any adaptive forecasting method is that the value of the exponential weighting constant within the extreme limits of zero and one, should increase in value as data become more changeable, and should decrease as data become more stable. This will satisfy the original argument for adaptive forecasting proposed at the beginning of this chapter because the forecasts, via the change in the value of the exponential smoothing constant, will alter in sympathy with changing data patterns. Having defined what is required of the exponential smoothing constant for adaptive forecasting, it is obvious that the modulus, or absolute value, of Trigg's original tracking signal fits all the requirements. It increases in value when data become more changeable; it decreases in value as data become more stable; and by definition it lies within the extreme limits of zero and one.

Hence, in a stationary situation, the forecast for any period in the future using the Trigg and Leach adaptive response rate forecasting model is given by:

$$f_{t+\tau} = \widetilde{u}_t = |T_t|d_t + (1 - |T_t|)\widetilde{u}_{t-1} \tag{5.1}$$

where, again,

$$\overline{e}_t = \alpha e_t + (1 - \alpha)\overline{e}_{t-1} \tag{5.2}$$

$$\text{MAD}_t = \alpha|e_t| + (1 - \alpha)\text{MAD}_{t-1} \tag{5.3}$$

and

$$T_t = \overline{e}_t/\text{MAD}_t \tag{5.4}$$

Using this method then, when forecasts tend to go out of control because of sudden changes in the data, the value of the tracking signal is automatically increased and therefore gives more weight to recent data, and the forecast 'homes' rapidly into the true average level. Once the system has settled at this level, the value of T_t is automatically reduced again to prevent the forecast responding to untypical fluctuations. This adaptive response rate method of forecasting produces a markedly improved response to sudden changes compared with simple

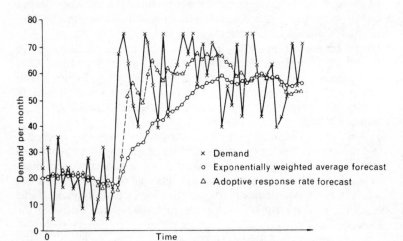

Fig. 5.3 Improved response of adaptive response rate forecast to step change in demand

exponentially weighted averages as shown in Fig. 5.3, and can also be adapted to linear and seasonal trend models.

Ironically, one slight disadvantage of this method is that, as forecasts are greatly improved forecasting errors are reduced, which in turn alters the values calculated for the tracking signal. In fact, this error reduction invalidates the use of the tracking signal (using the published values) for monitoring purposes when forecasts are of the adaptive response rate type as defined by equation (5.1). If the improved forecasts derived from adaptive response rate forecasting, and monitoring facilities are both required, this author[2] has suggested that a non-adaptive forecast must be generated simply to generate a value of the tracking signal for monitoring purposes.

Shone[3] has suggested a slight change to the Trigg-and-Leach formula which, it is claimed, reduces the response of the adaptive response rate forecast to spurious single period impulses, whilst maintaining the forecast's improved response to other types of changes.

Shone's modification is simply to use the one-period-delayed value of the tracking signal T_{t-1} rather than the current value T_t.

Then the adaptive rate response rate forecast for a stationary situation is given by

$$f_{t+\tau} = \widetilde{u}_t = |T_{t-1}|d_t + (1 - |T_{t-1}|)\widetilde{u}_{t-1} \tag{5.5}$$

and the characteristic of this type of adaptive response rate forecast compared with that defined by equation (5.1) is indicated in Fig. 5.4.

Appendix A, indicates in flow diagram form the necessary steps required to evaluate either the delayed or non-delayed versions of the adaptive response rate forecast.

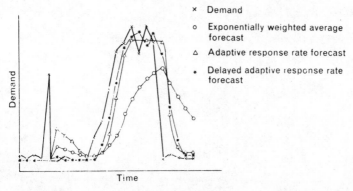

Fig. 5.4 Responses of exponentially weighted average, adaptive response rate, and delayed adaptive response rate forecasts to impulse and step changes in demand

References

1 CHOW, W.M. (1965) 'Adaptive control of the exponential smoothing constant', *Journal of Industrial Engineering*, 16, No. 5, 314
2 LEWIS, C.D. (1968) 'Viewpoints', *Operational Research Quarterly*, 19, No. 1, 96
3 SHONE, M.L. (1967) 'Viewpoints', *Operational Research Quarterly*, 18, No. 3, 318
4 THAMARA, T. (1968) *Exponential Smoothing with Automatic Weight Assignment*, San Francisco, paper presented at the TIMS/ORSA Joint National Meeting, May 1968
5 TRIGG, D.W. AND LEACH, A.G. (1967) 'Exponential smoothing with adaptive response rate', *Operational Research Quarterly*, 18, No. 1.

Exercise

Using Table 5.1. with $\alpha = 0.2$, evaluate the adaptive response rate forecast and delayed adaptive response rate forecast and show that the sums of squared forecasting errors are 3176 and 1986 respectively.

TABLE 5.1. Demand analysis/forecasting worksheet

1	Current demand value	d_t	55	50	58	49	86	52	54	49	58	68	75	78	82
2	Forecast	$f_t = u_{t-1}$	50*												
3	Error	$e_t = d_t - u_{t-1}$													
4	Squared error	e_t^2													
5	Cumulative squared error	Σe_t^2													
6	$\alpha \times$ error	αe_t													
7	$(1 - \alpha) \times$ past smoothed error	$(1-\alpha)\bar{e}_{t-1}$	0.0*												
8	Current smoothed error	$\bar{e}_t = \alpha e_t + (1-\alpha)\bar{e}_{t-1}$													
9	$\alpha \times$ absolute error	$\alpha |e_t|$													
10	$(1 - \alpha) \times$ past MAD	$(1-\alpha)MAD_{t-1}$													
11	Current MAD	$MAD_t = \alpha|e_t| + (1-\alpha)MAD_{t-1}$	4.0*												
12	Current std dev.	$\sigma_t = 1.25\ MAD_t$													
15	Tracking signal	$T_t = \bar{e}_t/MAD_t$													
14	Cumulative error	Σe_t													
15	Exponential weighting constant for forecast (see below)	α^1													
16	$\alpha^1 \times$ current demand	$\alpha^1 d_t$													
17	$(1 - \alpha^1) \times$ past forecast	$(1-\alpha^1)u_{t-1}$													
18	Next month's forecast	$f_{t+1} = u_t = \alpha^1 d_t + (1-\alpha^1)u_{t-1}$													

$\alpha = 0.1$ or 0.2; for adaptive response rate forecasting $\alpha^1 = |T_t|$; for delayed adaptive response rate forecasting $\alpha^1 = |T_{t-1}|$

*Estimate or guess

Chapter 6

Identification of data characteristics – the use of autocorrelation

When selecting an appropriate forecasting model, it is essential that the characteristics of the data being analysed should be established. Obviously, it would be unnecessarily expensive to use a sophisticated model, such as the Holt–Winter linear and seasonal additive model (described on page 32), when the data in question were stationary and simple exponential smoothing would have produced equally acceptable results at a fraction of the cost. Contrarily, were the data to contain linear growth and seasonal characteristics, simple exponential smoothing obviously would not be appropriate.

Because of the natural presence of random fluctuations or 'noise' in most industrial or business data, examination of the raw data by graphical means may very often *not* reveal the underlying characteristics making up the data, since these may well be obscured by the noise. Thus, what is required is an analysis technique or tool which will initially remove the camouflaging effect of the noise to reveal, and then subsequently identify, the characteristics present in the data.

Whilst several statistical methods of analysis have been proposed and are used to identify time series data characteristics, that technique now used predominantly in forecasting for the identification of trend characteristics is *autocorrelation analysis*.

Autocorrelation

Correlation is a statistical technique used to establish the relationship between one variable and another. In marketing, for instance, it might be possible to establish, to a greater or lesser extent, that a company's sales of a certain product were related to the investment in advertising for that product. If the relationship between sales and investment were proved to be very strong (highly correlated) it would be sensible to promote increased sales by making an increased advertising investment. However, if the relationship were proved to be weak (i.e. poorly or even negatively correlated) such increased investment would not be wise. (For further discussion on correlation and regression see Chapter 7.)

64

Whilst correlation measures the degree of relationship between two separate variables, autocorrelation (as the name itself suggests) measures the degree of self-relationship between a variable and itself. This apparent *non-sequitur* is achieved by using the original data as one series and the original data, lagged by a specified number of time periods, as the second series. Figure 6.1 indicates how monthly data

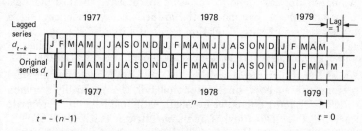

Fig. 6.1 Original and lagged series of monthly data

would be considered by autocorrelation analysis with the lag set equal to one period. In this situation January's observation is compared with February's, February's with March's etc., and in general d_{t-i} with d_{t-i-K} where K is the lag in time periods. The mathematical definition of the autocorrelation coefficient r_K at a lag of K is given by

$$r_K = \frac{\sum\limits_{t=0}^{n-1} (d_t - \bar{d}_t)(d_{t-K} - \bar{d}_{t-K})}{\sigma_{d_t} \cdot \sigma_{d_{t-K}}} \tag{6.1}$$

where

$$\sigma_{d_t} = \sqrt{\left(\frac{\sum\limits_{t=0}^{n-1} (d_t - \bar{d}_t)^2}{n-1} \right)} \tag{6.2}$$

and

$$\sigma_{d_{t-K}} = \sqrt{\left(\frac{\sum\limits_{t=0}^{n-1} (d_{t-K} - \bar{d}_{t-K})^2}{n-1} \right)} \tag{6.3}$$

and

d_t is the original series
d_{t-K} is the lagged series
$\bar{d}_t$ is the average of the original series
$\bar{d}_{t-K}$ is the average of the lagged series
n is the number of pairs of values being compared, which is reduced as the lag K increases.

The autocorrelation coefficient r_K can vary from +1 to −1. A value approaching +1 indicates a strong positive correlation between original data values and those lagged by K periods and would generally be associated with paired observations being close together. A large observation from the original series paired with a small observation from the lagged series would generally indicate negative correlation and r_K would, in this case, tend to −1. More specifically, for most practical purposes it can be assumed with 95 per cent confidence that a significant degree of autocorrelation exists at a lag of K if r_K exceeds a value of $\pm 2/\sqrt{n}$, i.e. approximately 0.6, 0.4, 0.3 and 0.3 for values of n of 12, 24, 36 and 48 respectively.

Whilst the reader might well be able to write a computer program to perform this analysis, since autocorrelation is a reasonably common statistical tool, most computer installations should have an appropriate package available. Increasingly forecasting software (such as the SIBYL/ RUNNER package of Makridakis and Wheelwright[1]) incorporates an autocorrelation analysis section.

First differencing

When a demand or sales series is subject to a linear additive trend, one way of removing that trend is to 'take first differences'. The taking of first differences is achieved by establishing a second series which is formed as the differences of the original series, as shown in Fig. 6.2. It is apparent from Fig. 6.2 that the average value of the first differences d_t^* (5 units) represents the rate of growth of the original series d_t.

Original series d_t	6		10		15		21		24		30		35		41
First differences $d_t^* = d_t - d_{t-1}$		4		5		6		3		6		5		6	

Fig. 6.2 The creation of first differences to remove the effect of an additive growth trend

The use of both autocorrelation analysis and first differencing is now demonstrated to identify time series subject to:

   (i)   no trend, i.e. a stationary situation (see Figs 1.1 or 6.3(a));
   (ii) a linear additive trend (aA) (see Figs 2.1 or 6.4(a));
   (iii) a pure seasonal trend (bA) (see Fig. 6.5(a));
   (iv) a linear and seasonal trend (cA) (see Figs 2.3 or 6.6(a)).

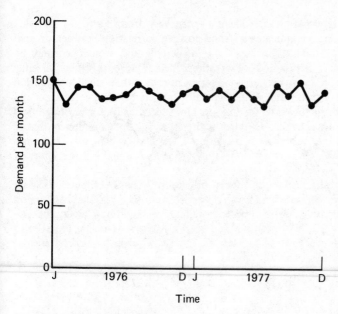

Fig. 6.3(a) Typical stationary data

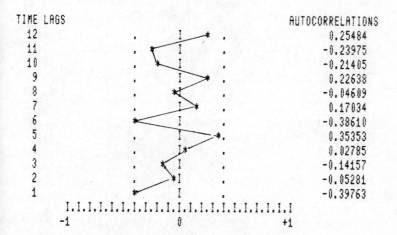

Fig. 6.3(b) Autocorrelogram of typical stationary data

68

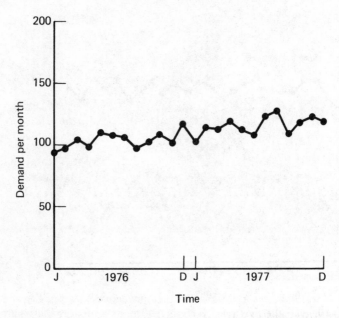

Fig. 6.4(a) Linear additive trend data (aA)

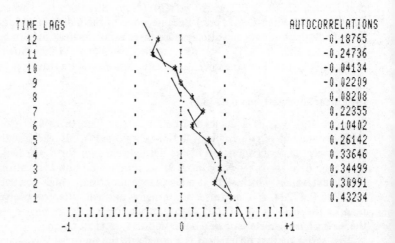

Fig. 6.4(b) Autocorrelogram of linear additive trend data (at *zero* differences)

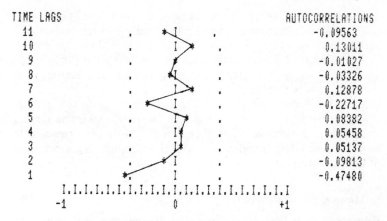

Fig. 6.4(c) Autocorrelogram of linear additive trend data (at *first* differences)

(i) Stationary data

Figure 6.3(a) indicates a stationary situation where the average demand per month over the two years is about 140 units a month, and whilst individual values vary about this average, there appears to be no growth or seasonality present. The autocorrelogram (i.e. plot of autocorrelation coefficients against respective time lags) for this situation is shown in Fig. 6.3(b). In Fig. 6.3(b) the dotted lines represent the plus and minus two standard error (i.e. 95 per cent confidence) limits of autocorrelation coefficients, $\pm2/\sqrt{n} = 0.2$ where $n = 24$. (Note. Strictly $n = 23$ when $K = 1$, $n = 22$ when $K = 2$, etc.) Because none of the individual values lie outside these limits, and also because there is no apparent pattern in the autocorrelation coefficients; such an autocorrelogram as that shown in Fig. 6.3(b) would be characteristic of any stationary data situation.

(ii) Linear additive trend data (aA)

Figure 6.4(a) depicts a demand situation where there is evidence of some linear additive growth over the two-year period. Whilst the growth is relatively small, examination of the autocorrelogram for this growth data Fig. 6.4b, shows a very marked pattern in the autocorrelation coefficient values which start at a lag of one month at a high positive value of 0.43234 and decrease uniformly until at a lag of twelve months the value is −0.18765. Such a strong linear pattern, angled to the vertical, is characteristic of a linear additive trend situation.

If a series of first differences is formed for the linear additive data shown in Fig. 6.4(a), the autocorrelogram for this new series would be as shown in Fig. 6.4(c). (Note. Because an analysis of the raw or original data can be considered as being an analysis at zero differences, such analyses are often referred to as such, i.e. Fig. 6.4(b)).

Examination of the autocorrelogram at first differences (Fig. 6.4(c)), where the linear additive trend of the original data has effectively been removed, reveals that there is now no strong trend apparent and that the first differences appear to be stationary since Fig. 6.3(b) and Fig. 6.4(c) are not dissimilar. An autocorrelation analysis which produces a strong linear pattern at zero differences (i.e. using the original data series) and no recognizable pattern at first differences, is characteristic of linear additive data.

(iii) Seasonal trend data (bB)

Figure 6.5(a) indicates four years of strongly seasonal data with summer and autumn peaks and winter and spring troughs. Remembering that four years of data is the minimum required to confidently define a seasonal pattern, it is apparent that when the autocorrelation lag is either twelve or 24; January values will be compared with January values of previous years, February with February, etc. Only for a seasonal situation would one expect strong positive correlation between demand or sales values drawn from the same calendar month but different years, and this is confirmed in the autocorrelogram (Fig. 6.5(b)). Here the values of the autocorrelation coefficients at lags of 12 and 24 months are respectively 0.54027 and 0.34421, both of which are significant (i.e. outside the 95 per cent confidence limits set equal to 0.3). This indicates a strong relationship between observations drawn from the same calendar month, but different years. Contrarily when the lag is either six or 18 months; when observations drawn from peak months are being compared with observations drawn from trough months, a strong negative correlation would be expected. This is confirmed with autocorrelation coefficients at lags of six and 18 months respectively of −0.67416 and −0.42020. A strong vertical pattern with many significantly large autocorrelation coefficients (such as that seen in Fig. 6.5(b)) is characteristic of a pure seasonal situation with no linear trend. (Note. Because the pattern in Fig. 6.5(b) is vertical, indicating that there is no linear trend, it is not really necessary to progress to an analysis at first differences.)

(iv) Linear and seasonal additive trend data (cA)

Figure 6.6(a) depicts four years of monthly demand data with apparent summer and autumn peaks and winter and spring troughs. As well as this seasonal element, there also appears to be evidence of small but

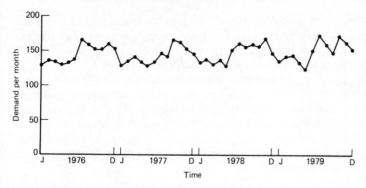

Fig. 6.5(a) Seasonal trend data

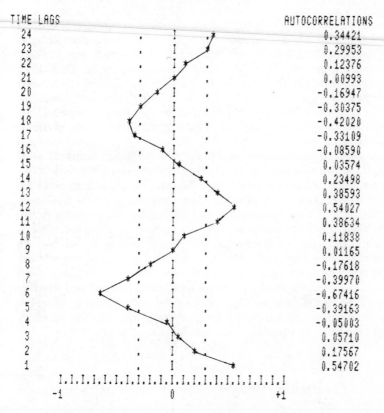

TIME LAGS		AUTOCORRELATIONS
24		0.34421
23		0.29953
22		0.12376
21		0.00993
20		-0.16947
19		-0.30375
18		-0.42020
17		-0.33109
16		-0.08590
15		0.03574
14		0.23498
13		0.38593
12		0.54027
11		0.38634
10		0.11838
9		0.01165
8		-0.17618
7		-0.39970
6		-0.67416
5		-0.39163
4		-0.05003
3		0.05710
2		0.17567
1		0.54702

-1   0   +1

Fig. 6.5(b) Autocorrelogram of seasonal trend data (at *zero* differences)

72

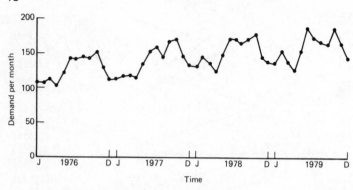

Fig. 6.6(a) Linear and seasonal additive trend data

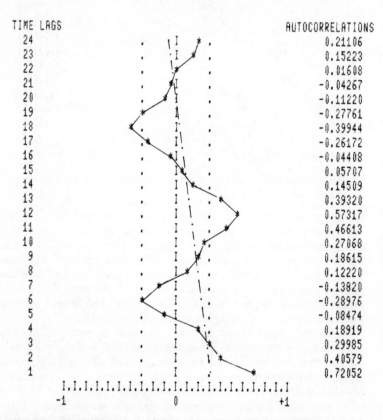

Fig. 6.6(b) Autocorrelogram of linear and seasonal additive trend data

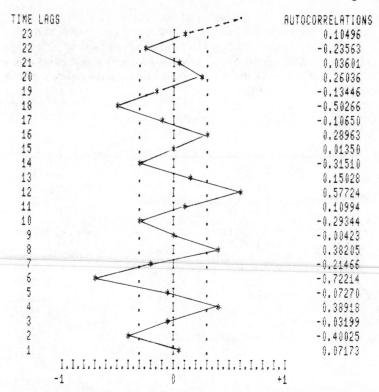

Fig. 6.6(c) Autocorrelogram of linear and seasonal data (at *first* differences)

steady growth. The autocorrelogram for these data (i.e. at zero differences), Fig. 6.6(b), reveals the strong seasonal pattern with significant positive correlation at a lag of 12 months and significant negative correlation at a lag of 18 months. The expected significant autocorrelation at six and 24 months does not occur because the whole pattern is angled from top left to bottom right — as a result of the slight linear growth evidenced in the original data. This angled seasonal pattern is typical of linear and seasonal additive trend data.

When the trend effect for this situation is removed by first differencing, the resultant autocorrelogram (Fig. 6.6(c)) produces a pattern that can be seen to lie vertically and although the overall seasonal pattern now looks somewhat different, close examination reveals that the shape is similar between lags one to 12 and 13 to 24 (this latter value having been inserted manually simply because it has been excluded by the computer program). In this situation the number of autocorrelation coefficients that lie outside the 95 per cent confidence limits again reveals the significance of the seasonal element.

These four examples of typical situation experienced in industrial and business data, with their associated autocorrelograms at either zero or first differences indicate how autocorrelation analysis can be used to identify data characteristics.

References

1 MAKRIDAKIS, S. AND WHEELWRIGHT, S.C. (1977) *Interactive Forecasting* Palo Alto, The Scientific Press

Bibliography

BRYANT, E.C. (1960) *Statistical Analysis* New York, McGraw-Hill
MAKRIDAKIS, S. AND WHEELWRIGHT, S.C. (1978) *Forecasting Methods and Applications* New York, Wiley
MONTGOMERY, D.C. AND JOHNSON, L.A. (1976) *Forecasting and Time Series Analysis* New York, McGraw-Hill

Section 2

Medium-term forecasting
(regression and curve fitting)

Introduction

Medium-term forecasting is generally, although not exclusively concerned with:

(i) annual data, which in many situations may be extracted from published statistics;

(ii) situations where the producing of forecasts may be a once-off exercise which need not necessarily be repeated, much less continually updated;

(iii) situations where forecasts are required for relatively few data series;

(iv) situations where forecasts are *not* often linked to a particular item or product but are more general in nature might be in applications such as: a capital investment programme, market sector analysis, and profit forecasting.

For such applications it is apparent that forecasting models can be relatively sophisticated and, thus, more expensive to operate than those described for short-term forecasting applications in Section 1.

The technique of linear regression, which essentially fits a straight line to a series of observed values, is a proven and well established statistical method. Its emergence as a technique which can be used for linear and non-linear curve fitting has really only come about with the development of fast and cheap computing facilities with the ability to perform the simple but multitudinous calculations required by the method. It is this development which has established regression and curve fitting methods as a major forecasting technique.

Forecasting models based on linear regression methods or its derivatives:

(i) generally require more data than exponential smoothing models to produce sensible forecasts;

(ii) cannot be updated, other than by performing a further complete analysis when more data become available;

(iii) are totally inappropriate for seasonal forecasting;

(iv) provide more information concerning the suitability of the forecasting model.

In this section on medium-term forecasting, Chapter 7 describes the basic theory behind linear regression (known as trend analysis when the independent variable is time) and Chapter 8 describes how, by suitable transformations of either or both the data (the dependent variable) and time (the independent variable), the linear regression model can be extended to fit a family of non-linear curves. Chapter 9 describes precedures for fitting curves based on the modified exponential equation rather than the equation of a straight line, as in linear regression. Finally, Chapter 10 examines the use of a technique known as the V-MASK/CUSUM test as a method of monitoring medium-term forecasts.

Because regression techniques have developed largely from within the discipline of statistical theory, and also because the independent variable need not be constrained to take sequential values of equal increments, as occurs in a time series where $t = 1, 2, 3, 4$, etc. (i.e. an independent variable x could take sequential values 3.1, 2.2, 6.0, 4.0, etc.), the convention of subscripts is usually different from that used in short-term forecasting (see page 4). When using regression methods for time series analysis (sometimes this particular method is called trend analysis) it is assumed that at any time t one has available n observations of the dependent variable y (i.e. sales per annum, yearly profit) etc. and that the oldest observation is y_1 and the most recent observation y_n. This system of subscripting can be clearly seen in Fig. 7.1.

As with short-term forecasting, however, the forecast horizon is assumed to be τ periods ahead of the current or most recent observation.

(Note. Through this section the summation sign Σ is assumed to represent a summation from 1 to n (i.e. $\sum_{t=1}^{n}$) unless otherwise stated.)

Chapter 7

Linear regression (trend analysis)

Presented with a series of observations plotted on a graph, a logical approach to forecasting future values would be to *fit* a straight line to the sample data in such a way as to obtain a reasonable spread of observations either side of the line and then to extrapolate (i.e. extend) that line to produce forecasts. Whilst such line fitting for forecasting purposes appears to be a logical approach (and few readers could deny they have not done it in the past) on detailed examination the method can be shown to be fraught with difficulties, some of which are:

(i) Would such a straight line necessarily be a good fit to the data and on what subjective basis does the observer assess the goodness of the fit; equal number of points either side of the line — or what?

(ii) Whilst such a straight line might be a good fit, and authors of statistical texts on regression do tend to over-exaggerate the inability to produce a good fit by graphical methods, it does not necessarily follow that a well-fitted line can then be extrapolated to produce sensible forecasts.

(iii) The straight line is only one of many curves (technically a straight line is a linear curve) which could be fitted to a time series and it is, therefore, unlikely to always be the best curve. One chooses a straight line mainly for ease of drawing rather than for suitability of fitting.

However, since the equations of many curves can be transposed to the equation of a straight line, the 'best' way of fitting a straight line does have wide implications and will, therefore, be considered in detail.

Fitting the best straight line — the regression equation

Although it is beyond the scope of this text, it can be shown[1] that the 'best' fit of a straight line of the form

$$\hat{y}_t = a + bt \tag{7.1}$$

where $\hat{y}_t$ is the calculated value at time t of a dependent variable y,

79

and a and b are constants, occurs when the sum of *squared* errors is a minimum. These errors are defined as the difference between actual values of the dependent variable y, namely y_t, and computed values $\hat{y}_t$, i.e. $y_t - \hat{y}_t$. It can be shown relatively easily[1,2] that the values of parameters a and b of the straight line required to minimize the sum of squared errors $\Sigma(y_t - \hat{y}_t)^2$ are given by:

$$b = \frac{n\Sigma t\, y_t - \Sigma t \Sigma y_t}{n\Sigma t^2 - (\Sigma t)^2} \qquad (7.2)$$

where b is referred to as the coefficient of regression (not to be confused with the correlation coefficient) and represents the slope of the regression line and Σ is assumed to be $\overset{n}{\underset{t=1}{\Sigma}}$ here and throughout this chapter, and

$$a = \frac{\Sigma y_t - b\Sigma t}{n} \qquad (7.3)$$

where a is the intercept on the y axis, i.e. $\hat{y}_t$ at time $t = 0$.

An example of the fitting of a regression line (using equations (7.2) and (7.3)) is shown in Fig. 7.1. In this example, figures for eleven years (1967–1977) of UK Central and Local Government annual

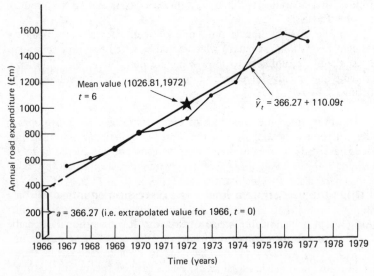

Fig. 7.1 Regression line fitted to road expenditure data

TABLE 7.1. Calculations required to find the regression line for annual road expenditure (£m) 1967–1977 (Source :Transport Statistics Great Britain 1967–1977 (1979) Government Statistical Service)

Year	t	t^2	y_t	y_t^2	ty_t
1967	1	1	560	313 600	560
1968	2	4	608	369 664	1216
1969	3	9	685	469 225	2055
1970	4	16	807	651 249	3228
1971	5	25	839	703 921	4195
1972	6	36	914	835 396	5484
1973	7	49	1100	1 210 000	7700
1974	8	64	1196	1 430 416	9568
1975	9	81	1490	2 247 001	13 491
1976	10	100	1574	2 477 476	15 740
1977	11	121	1513	2 289 169	16 643
	$\Sigma t = 66$	$\Sigma t^2 = 506$	$\Sigma y_t = 11\,295$	$\Sigma y_t^2 = 12\,997\,117$	$\Sigma ty_t = 79\,880$

$$b = \frac{n \, \Sigma \, ty_t - \Sigma t \, \Sigma y_t}{n \, \Sigma \, t^2 - (\Sigma t)^2} = \frac{11(79880) - 66(11295)}{11(506) - (66)^2}$$

$$= \frac{878680 - 745470}{5566 - 4356} = \frac{133210}{1210} = \underline{110.09}$$

$$a = \frac{\Sigma y_t}{n} - \frac{b \Sigma t}{n} = \frac{11295}{11} - \frac{110.09(66)}{11}$$

$$= 1026.81 - 660.54 = \underline{366.27}$$

expenditure on roads have been analysed. The necessary calculations are shown in Table 7.1 and produce the following equation for the regression line:

$$\hat{y}_t = 366.27 + 110.09t$$

It should be noted that this and all regression lines always pass through the mean value $(\bar{y}, \bar{t})$ which in this case is (1026.81, 1972).

Although on paper, these calculations look somewhat formidable, in computer terms they are trivial and can even be pre-programmed on relatively cheap hand-held calculators. (Note. Regression analysis can examine the relationship between two variables which need not be in the form of a time series, i.e. the independent variable need not be time and thus incremented in equal steps. When applied specifically to time series the technique is sometimes termed 'trend analysis'.)

The sources of variation in regression analysis

To determine the significance of a regression analysis it is necessary to examine how well the regression equation explains the variation of the dependent variable y in terms of t as compared with the total or overall variation of y (independent of t).

Total variation

The variation of a series of observations is measured as the sum of squared differences (or deviations) between individual observations and the average for all observations. In this case the total variation of y will be given by

$$\text{total variation} = \Sigma(y_t - \bar{y})^2 \tag{7.4}$$

where

$$\bar{y} = \frac{\Sigma y_t}{n} \tag{7.5}$$

For computational convenience, it can be shown that equation (7.4) simplifies to

$$\text{total variation} = \Sigma y_t^2 - \frac{(\Sigma y_t)^2}{n} \tag{7.6}$$

and for the road expenditure data considered in Table 7.1:

$$\text{total variation} = (12997117 - 11295^2/11)$$
$$= 1399205.64$$

Variation explained by (i.e. due to) regression

It is evident that if there is a mathematical relationship between y and t, much of the *total* variation will be explained by the regression line. If there is no such relationship, none of the *total* variation of y will be explained by the regression line.

The variation of y explained by the regression line is measured as the sum of squared errors between calculated values $\hat{y}_t$ and the average for y, namely $\bar{y}$ (defined by equation (7.5)), and this variation would, therefore, be given by

$$\text{variation due to regression} = \Sigma(\hat{y}_t - \bar{y})^2 \tag{7.7}$$

which for computational purposes can be shown to be

$$\text{variation due to regression} = b^2 \left(\Sigma t^2 - \frac{(\Sigma t)^2}{n} \right) \tag{7.8}$$

or, alternatively,

variation due to regression $= a\Sigma y_t + b\Sigma t\, y_t - \dfrac{(\Sigma y_t)^2}{n}$ (7.9)

Hence, for the road expenditure data in Table 7.1, using equation (7.8):

variation due to regression $= 110.09^2\ (506 - 66^2/11)$
$= 1333178.89$

Residual variation

The variation not explained by the regression line is known as the residual variation and is defined as the sum of squared differences of the observations y_t about the regression line $\hat{y}_t$, hence

residual variation $= \Sigma(y_t - \hat{y}_t)^2$ (7.10)

For computational purposes the residual variation is generally calculated simply as the difference between the total variation and the variation due to regression. Thus for the road expenditure data

Residual variation $=$ Total variation $-$ variation due to regression
$= 1399205.64 - 1333178.89 = 66026.75$

However, if it is required to calculate the residual variation directly from source data, it can be shown that

$\Sigma(y_t - \hat{y}_t)^2 = \Sigma y_t^2 - a\Sigma y_t - b\Sigma ty_t$ (7.11)

and as a crosscheck, for the road expenditure data

$\Sigma(y_t - \hat{y}_t)^2 = 12997117 - 366.27\,(11295) - 110.9\,(79880)$
$= 66006.00$

TABLE 7.2. Sources of variation in regression analysis

Source of variation	Description	Sum of squares
Due to regression	Variation of dependent variable y explained by the regression line $\hat{y}_t$	$b^2\,[\Sigma t^2 - (\Sigma t)^2/n]$ or $a\Sigma y_t + b\Sigma t\, y_t - (\Sigma y_t^2)/n$
Residual	Variation of dependent variable y *not* explained by regression line $\hat{y}_t$, i.e. variation of y remaining around the regression line	$\Sigma y_t^2 - a\Sigma y_t - b\Sigma ty_t$
Total	Total or overall variation of the dependent variable y	$\Sigma y_t^2 - (\Sigma y_t)^2/n$

which is a mere 20.75 (i.e. 0.03 per cent) low because of the earlier rounding of a and b to two decimal places.

A summary defining and describing the sources of variation in regression analysis is shown in Table 7.2.

Correlation coefficient r and index of determination r^2

In general terms the correlation coefficient r, which varies between $+1$ and -1, is a measure of the relationship between two variables; more specifically in the time series case between the dependent variable

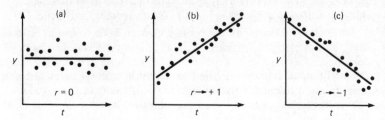

Fig. 7.2 Times series with different correlation coefficients r

y and independent variable time (t). Figure 7.2 shows three different situations where:

(a) $r = 0$; there is no correlation between y and t

(b) $r \rightarrow +1$; there is a strong positive correlation between y and t and therefore, increases in t can be assumed to cause increases in y.

(c) $r \rightarrow -1$; there is a strong negative correlation between y and t and increases in t can be assumed to cause *decreases* in y.

The index of determination r^2 (i.e. the correlation coefficient squared) is defined as the proportion of total variation explained by the regression line, hence

$$r^2 = \frac{\text{variation due to regression}}{\text{total variation}}$$

which for computational purposes becomes, using equation (7.8),

$$r^2 = \frac{b^2\left[\Sigma t^2 - (\Sigma t)^2/n\right]}{\Sigma y_t^2 - (\Sigma y_t)^2/n} \tag{7.12}$$

Both the index of determination r^2 and correlation coefficient r are important measures in medium-term forecasting systems, and although the correlation coefficient is used more widely, since both appear in the associated literature, software, etc., to avoid confusion the following points should be noted:

(i) Whilst r^2, the index of determination, is always positive the correlation coefficient r conventionally adopts the sign of b, the co-efficient of regression. The polarity of the sign preceeding the correlation coefficient r simply indicates the type of relationship or association of y on t (see Fig. 7.2). A situation where $r = -0.86$ would indicate a higher (though negative) degree of correlation than one where $r = 0.68$

(ii) It is the coefficient of determination r^2 which defines the pro-portion of total variation explained by the regression line (see equation (7.11)) *not* the correlation coefficient r. Thus although a value of $r = 0.7$ might look encouraging, in fact with a corresponding index of determination of $r^2 = 0.49$ the inference must be that less than half the total variation is explained by the regression line.

Since both measures are always less than or equal to one, it follows that the correlation coefficient is always greater than the index of determination (i.e. $r > r^2$) other than where both are equal to one. This must mean that the variation explained by the regression line as a proportion of the total variation will always be less than r.

(iii) The significance of both r and r^2 depends on n, the number of

TABLE 7.3. Values of r and r^2 which should be achieved if regression line is to be used for forecasting. (These values represent a 90 per cent level of confidence.)

Number of observations n	Value of correlation coefficient r	Value of index of determination r^2
5	0.58	0.34
6	0.55	0.30
7	0.52	0.27
8	0.50	0.25
9	0.48	0.23
10	0.46	0.21
15	0.39	0.15
20	0.34	0.12
25	0.31	0.10
30	0.29	0.08
35	0.27	0.07
40	0.25	0.06
45	0.23	0.05
50	0.22	0.05
60	0.20	0.04
70	0.19	0.04
80	0.18	0.03
90	0.17	0.03
100	0.16	0.03

observations being considered. When n is low a high degree of association of the sample data with time is necessary for forecasts to be meaningful. Table 7.3 gives the values of r and r^2 (for corresponding values of n) which must be achieved if forecasts based on the regression line equation are to be viewed with any confidence.

For the road expenditure data shown in Fig. 7.2, whose sources of variation have already been analysed, it follows that the index of determination is given by

$$r^2 = \frac{\text{variation due to regression}}{\text{total variation}} = \frac{1333178.89}{1399205.64}$$

$$= 0.95$$

or

$$r = 0.98$$

The correlation coefficient r is considered to be positive since b, the coefficient of regression, has also been found to be positive ($b = 110.09$, see page 81).

It is apparent that in this case the index of determination $r^2 = 0.95$, evaluated from eleven observations, exceeds by far that required (see Table 7.3) and hence, the regression line equation can be sensibly used for forecasting.

Forecasting using regression line and the importance of the confidence interval

Forecasting using the regression line equation is simply a matter of substituting the correct value of t in the regression equation

$$\hat{y}_t = a + bt \tag{7.13}$$

and evaluating the results.

For the road expenditure data (which have been progressively analysed throughout this chapter) to produce a forecast for 1978 one recognizes that for that year $t = 12$ and, hence

$$\hat{y}_{12} = 366.27 + 110.09\,(12)$$

$$= 1687.35$$

were one to adopt the normal forecasting convention, namely that the most recent observed value (i.e. that in 1977) occurred at time t and forecasts were for τ periods ahead, it follows that in equation (7.13), $t = n + \tau$.

Confidence interval

It must be remembered that whilst a forecast is the unbiased estimate of expected future values, unless the forecast can be qualified by defining the limits either side of it within which one can confidently expect actual future values to fall, the forecast by itself is virtually meaningless.

In regression analysis these limits are defined by the confidence interval, this being the interval (i.e. distance either side of the forecast) that one would expect, with a specified degree of confidence, actual future values to fall within. Thus a forecast of 1000 associated with a 95 per cent confidence interval of ± 100 would mean that one could expect, with 95 per cent confidence, future values to be between 900 and 1100. The same forecast with a 95 per cent confidence interval of ±1000, however, should be interpreted as indicating that future values could fall anywhere between 0 and 2000.

In regression analysis, the size of the confidence interval is a minimum at the average value $(\bar{y}, \bar{t})$ of the sample data, and increases the further away from the average value its computation occurs.

To evaluate the confidence interval for any particular forecast, it is first necessary to know the standard error of regression S_r (sometimes referred to as the standard error of estimate). The standard error of regression is defined as the square-root of the mean squared deviations of actual observations y_t around the regression line $\hat{y}_t$ hence

$$S_r = \sqrt{\left(\frac{\Sigma(y_t - \hat{y}_t)^2}{n - 2}\right)} \qquad (7.14)$$

(Note. The $n - 2$ divisor in equation (7.13) results from theoretically losing two degrees of freedom, calculating $\bar{y}$ and the other value of $\hat{y}_t$ to establish the regression line.)

Having established S_r, the standard error of regression, it can be shown that the standard error of the forecasts $S\hat{y}_t$ is given by

$$S\hat{y}_t = S_r \sqrt{\left(1 + \frac{1}{n} + \frac{(t - \bar{t})^2}{\Sigma(t - \bar{t})^2}\right)} \qquad (7.15)$$

which can be seen to be a function of: (i) $1/n$, the reciprocal of the number of observations n, thus if n is very large $1/n$ tends to zero; (ii) $(t - \bar{t})$, the distance (in time periods) from the average of the sample data at which the forecast is being calculated.

Readers are reminded that for computational purposes, the residual variation $\Sigma(y_t - \hat{y}_t)^2$ required in the calculation of S_r (equation (7.14)) can either be evaluated as the difference between total variation and variation due to regression or directly from source data using equations (7.10) or (7.11). Also, if the usual forecasting time convention is adhered to, which assumes that the most recent observation in the sample data occurred at time t and forecasts are being made for τ periods ahead, it follows that $(t - \bar{t})$ can be replaced by $[\tau + \dfrac{(n-1)}{2}]$ in equation (7.15). By introducing both these changes and incorporating equation (7.14) in (7.15), the standard error of forecasts $S\hat{y}_{t+\tau}$ can be defined as

$$S\hat{y}_{t+\tau} = \sqrt{\left(\frac{\Sigma y_t^2 - a\Sigma y_t - b\Sigma t\, y_t}{n-2}\right)}\sqrt{\left(1 + \frac{1}{n} + \frac{\left[\tau + \frac{(n-1)}{2}\right]^2}{\Sigma t^2 - (\Sigma t)^2/n}\right)}$$

(7.16)

Having established the stand error of forecasts, the 99, 95 and 68 per cent confidence intervals are defined as $\pm 3S\hat{y}_{t+\tau}$, $\pm 2S\hat{y}_{t+\tau}$ and $\pm S\hat{y}_{t+\tau}$ respectively.

For the road expenditure data, accepting previously calculated

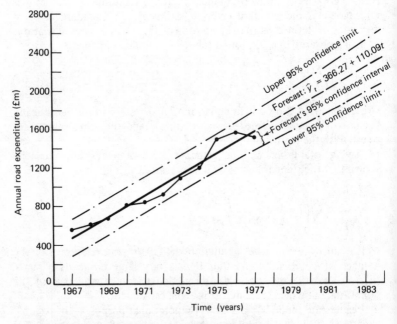

Fig. 7.3 Forecasts for road expenditure together with 95 per cent confidence limits

TABLE 7.4. Tabulation of upper and lower confidence interval for road expenditure time data

Year	τ	$\sqrt{\left(1+\dfrac{1}{n}+\dfrac{\left[\tau+\dfrac{(n-1)}{2}\right]^2}{\Sigma(t-\bar{t})^2}\right)}$	Calculated values and forecasts y_t	Actual values y_t	95% confidence interval	
					Lower	Upper
1967	0*	1.15	476.36	560	279.39	673.33
1968	−1*	1.11	586.46	608	396.34	776.58
1969	−2*	1.08	696.55	685	511.57	881.53
1970	−3*	1.06	806.64	807	625.08	988.20
1971	−4*	1.05	916.73	839	736.89	1096.57
1972($\bar{t}$)	−5	1.04	1026.82	914	848.69	1204.95
1973	−4	1.05	1136.91	1100	957.07	1316.75
1974	−3	1.06	1247.00	1196	1065.44	1428.55
1975	−2	1.08	1357.09	1499	1172.11	1542.07
1976	−1	1.11	1467.18	1574	1277.06	1657.30
1977	0	1.15	1577.27	1513	1380.30	1774.24
1978	1	1.19	1687.35		1483.56	1891.20
1979	2	1.24	1797.45		1585.06	2009.84
1980	3	1.29	1907.55		1686.60	2128.50
1981	4	1.35	2017.64		1786.41	2248.87
1982	5	1.41	2127.73		1886.23	2369.23
1983	6	1.48	2237.82		1983.51	2490.49
1984	7	1.55	2347.91		2082.43	2613.39

*Since the confidence interval is symmetrical about $\bar{t}$, using the normal *forecasting* time convention, below $\bar{t}$ τ must be set equal to −$(n-1+\tau)$ in equation (7.16). However, in practice it is never necessary to calculate confidence intervals below $\bar{t}$ for forecasting purposes.

results, for the one-period ahead forecast for 1978 one obtains for $\tau = 1$:

$$S\hat{y}_{t+1} = \sqrt{\left(\frac{66006}{9}\right)}\sqrt{\left(1 + \frac{1}{11} + \frac{(1+5)^2}{110}\right)}$$

$$= 85.64 \, \sqrt{(1 + 0.09 + 0.33)}$$

$$= 85.64 \, (1.19) = 101.91$$

From which one can deduce that the 95 per cent confidence interval for the 1978 forecast of 1687.35 would be defined by 1687.38 ± 2(101.91), i.e. producing a lower limit of 1483.56 and an upper limit of 1891.20.

Table 7.4 tabulates the values of the 95 per cent confidence limits for the road expenditure data and Fig. 7.3 shows these confidence limits plotted either side of the regression line — extrapolated to produce forecasts up to 1984, perhaps a propitious year at which to stop!

Linear regression analysis (or trend analysis when applied particularly to time series) is a very powerful technique for producing medium-term forecasts. The technique not only produces forecasts but examines the validity of those forecasts in relation to the data being analysed. Having confirmed that the forecasts being produced are valid, the technique quantifies 'the envelope' around the forecast within which actual future values will occur with a specified degree of confidence.

In addition to these features, regression analysis is used as a basis for more general curve-fitting, as is described in Chapter 8.

Appendix E is a flow diagram which indicates the necessary logic and calculations required to establish the values of the regression coefficients a and b and calculated values $\hat{y}_t$.

References

1. BRYANT, E.C. (1960) *Statistical Analysis* New York, McGraw-Hill
2. HALSTEAD, H.J. (1960) *Introduction to Statistical Methods* London, Macmillan

Bibliography

WHEELWRIGHT, S.C. AND MAKRIDAKIS, S. (1973) *Forecasting Methods for Management* New York, Wiley
YEOMANS, K.A. (1968) *Introducing Statistics − Statistics for the Social Scientist* Vol 1, Harmondsworth, Penguin

Exercise

The data shown below represent the UK expenditure on road vehicles for the years 1967–1977 (Source: Government Statistical Service (1979) 'Transport Statistics Great Britain 1967–1977')

Year	1967	1968	1969	1970	1971	1972	1973	1974	1975	1976	1977
Expenditure (£m)	1008	1129	1087	1164	1628	1971	2104	1969	2388	3190	3993

For these sample data, confirm that . . .

(i)   the regression coefficient b (= 265.07);
(ii) the regression line constant a (= 376.02);
(iii) the correlation coefficient r (= 0.93);
(iv) the minimum standard error of forecasts $S_{\hat{y}_\tau}$ (= 368.71);
(v)   the forecast of expenditure on vehicles for 1978; y_1 (= 3556.89, at $\tau = 1$ or $t = 12$);
(vi) the 95 per cent confidence interval for y_1 (= 2679.36 to 4434.42).

Chapter 8

Curve fitting–curves that can be expressed by the equation of a straight line

If any equation of a curve can be transposed into the general form of a straight line

$$\hat{y}_t = a + bt$$

it is possible to use the least squares fitting procedure described in Chapter 7 to calculate the relevant parameters a and b and to then use the equation of the curve to produce forecasts.

The two most commonly used transformations used in curve fitting are natural logarithms ($\log_e$) and reciprocals ($1/t$).

In time series application it is obviously possible to transform either the dependent variable y_t or the independent variable t, or both. When only one variable is transformed this form of transformation is sometimes referred to as 'semi-' (i.e. semi-logarithmic) and when both variables are transformed 'double-' (i.e. double-reciprocal).

In this chapter the eight possible curves deriving from combinations of transformations of the dependent variable y_t and the independent variable t, using both natural logarithmic and reciprocal transformations, will be individually investigated.

Informed statistical opinion[5] doubts the validity of taking transformations of the independent variable *time* on the basis that such transformations cannot be sensibly interpreted in real life. In spite of this, curves which are based on transformations of time are regularly incorporated in most computer curve fitting packages[4] and are included here for completeness.

The basic theory behind the 'linearization' of each curve will be explained and each curve will be fitted to the road expenditure data analysed in Chapter 7. This will enable those readers developing their own fitting programs to check their results.

The responses of these eight different curves to the road expenditure data are also recorded in Table 8.10 which indicates the rankings of the fitting performance of the curves in terms of index of determination (r^2), mean squared error (MSE) and mean absolute percentage error

TABLE 8.1. Curves that can be transposed to a straight line by suitable transformations

Curve name	Equation	Transformations	Basic Shape
Linear	$\hat{y}_t = a + bt$	None	
Exponential (simple)	$\hat{y}_t = ae^{bt}$	$Y_t = \log_e y_t$	b>0, b<0
Power	$\hat{y}_t = at^b$	$Y_t = \log_e y_t$ $T = \log_e t$	b<0, b>0
Hyperbolic (i)	$\hat{y}_t = a + b/t$	$T = 1/t$	b>0, b<0, $t = b/a$
Hyperbolic (ii)	$\hat{y}_t = 1/(a + bt)$	$Y_t = 1/y_t$	b>0, b<0, $t = a/b$
Hyperbolic (iii) or simple rational	$\hat{y}_t = t/(a + bt)$	$Y_t = 1/y_t$ $T = 1/t$	$\frac{1}{b}$, b>0, b<0, $t = a/b$
Logarithmic	$\hat{y}_t = a + b \log_e t$	$T = \log_e t$	
S	$\hat{y}_t = e^{a + b/t}$	$Y_t = \log_e t$ $T = 1/t$	b> -a, e^a, b< -a
Inverse log	$\hat{y}_t = \dfrac{1}{a + b \log_e t}$	$Y_t = 1/y_t$ $T = \log_e t$	b>0, $\frac{1}{a}$, b<0, $a/b > \log_e t$

(MAPE). Finally, at the end of the chapter, the choosing of a possible 'best' curve using a generalized curve fitting package will be discussed.

The eight curves to be investigated in this chapter together with their equations, necessary transformations and basic shape are shown in Table 8.1.

The simple exponential curve

The simple exponential curve is defined by the equation

$$\hat{y}_t = ae^{bt} \tag{8.1}$$

where e = 2.71828.
(Note. Two alternative forms of the exponential curve are

$$\hat{y}_t = \begin{cases} e^{a' + bt} & \text{where } a' = \log_e a \\ ab'e^t & \text{where } b' = \text{antilog}_e b \end{cases}$$

Taking natural logarithms of both sides of equation (8.1) one obtains

$$\log_e \hat{y}_t = \log_e a + bt \log_e e \tag{8.2}$$

which, knowing that $\log_e e = 1$ and introducing a transformed dependent variable $y_t = \log_e y_t$, becomes

$$\hat{y}_t = a' + bt \tag{8.3}$$

In this form values of a (= $\text{antilog}_e a'$) and b can be evaluated using normal linear regression procedures (see Table 8.2 for road expenditure data application) such that calculated values of the dependent variable $\hat{y}_t$ can be evaluated using equation (8.1). The resulting curve is shown in Fig. 8.1 in which forecasts for two periods ahead have also been produced, the forecast for 1978 being given by $\hat{y}_{12} = 496.21e^{(0.111)12}$ = 1879.9.

The simple exponential curve is very important because it specifies that the *rate* of growth (if $b > 0$) is constant at any point in time.

TABLE 8.2. Calculations required to fit exponential curve to road expenditure data

Variable	Dependent	Independent		
Form	$Y_t = \log_e y_t$	t		
$n = 11$	$\Sigma y_t = 75.60$ $\Sigma Y_t^2 = 520.91$	$\Sigma t = 66$ $\Sigma t^2 = 506$	$\Sigma t\, Y_t = 465.76$	

$$b = \frac{n\Sigma t Y_t - \Sigma t \, \Sigma Y_t}{n\Sigma t^2 - (\Sigma t)^2} = \frac{11(465.76) - 66(75.60)}{11(506) - (66)^2} = 0.111$$

$$a' = \frac{\Sigma Y_t - b\Sigma t}{n} = \frac{(75.60) - 0.111\,(66)}{11} = 6.207$$

therefore

$$a = \text{antilog}_e\ 6.207 = 496.21$$

$$\hat{y}_t = 496.21e^{0.111\, t}$$

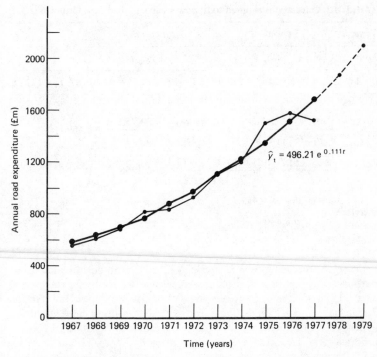

Fig. 8.1 Fitted exponential curve and forecasts for road expenditure data

Thus it is the curve which relates closely to inflation, where the co-efficient b represents the rate of inflation. With 20 per cent inflation (i.e. $b = 0.2$) values more than double in three years and quadruple in seven. Whilst such compound growth (i.e. unit increases in time t being accompanied by fixed proportional increases in the dependent variable y_t) cannot often be sustained for long periods, over a period of three to four years such a curve can provide a good fit. The exponential curve is used extensively in economics and has also featured in ecological models[2].

The power curve

The basic power curve is defined by the equation

$$\hat{y}_t = at^b \tag{8.4}$$

Taking natural logarithms of both sides of equation (8.4), one obtains

$$\log_e \hat{y}_t = \log_e a + b\log_e t \tag{8.5}$$

TABLE 8.3. Calculations required to fit power curve to road expenditure data

Variable	Dependent	Independent
Form	$Y_t = \log_e y_t$	$T \log_e t$

$n = 11$ $\Sigma Y_t = 75.60$ $\Sigma Y_t^2 = 520.91$ $\Sigma T = 17.50$ $\Sigma T^2 = 33.40$ $\Sigma T Y_t = 122.88$

$$b = \frac{n \Sigma TY_t - \Sigma T \Sigma Y_t}{n \Sigma T^2 - (\Sigma T)^2} = \frac{11(122.88) - 17.50(75.60)}{11(33.40) - (17.5)^2} = 0.469$$

$$a' = \frac{\Sigma Y_t - b\Sigma T}{n} = \frac{(75.60) - 0.469\,(17.5)}{11} = 6.1266$$

$$a = \text{antilog}_e\, a' = 457.9$$

therefore

$$\hat{y}_t = 457.9 t^{0.469}$$

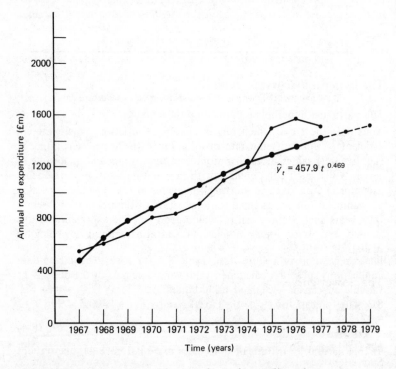

Fig. 8.2 Fitted power curve and forecasts for road expenditure data

If logarithmic transforms of the dependent variable $\hat{y}_t$ and independent variable t are introduced as $\hat{y}_t = \log_e \hat{y}_t$ and $T = \log_e t$ respectively, equation (8.5) becomes

$$\hat{y}_t = a' + bT \tag{8.6}$$

In this form values of a (= antilog$_e$ a') and b can be evaluated using normal linear regression procedures (see Table 8.3 for road expenditure data application) such that calculated values and forecasts of the original dependent variable $\hat{y}_t$ can be evaluated using equation (8.4) as illustrated in Fig. 8.2. The forecast for 1978 ($t = 12$) is given by $\hat{y}_{12} = 457.9 \, (12)^{0.469} = 1468.6$.

The power curve can exhibit slopes that are continually increasing or decreasing when b is positive but only slopes which are decreasing when b is negative. A special situation arises when $b = -1$ and $\hat{y}_t = a/t$. This relationship defines a rectangular hyperbola within which the product of the coordinates on the curve are constant (i.e. $t\,\hat{y}_t = a$). In economics this can be shown to be the condition required of a demand curve possessing unit elasticity throughout its length, i.e. percentage *increases* in time t cause equal percentage *decreases* in the dependent variable $\hat{y}_t$.

The hyperbolic curve — type (i)

This particular hyperbola is defined by the equation

$$\hat{y}_t = a + b/t \tag{8.7}$$

and can be transposed into a linear equation simply by introducing a reciprocal transformation of the independent variable t, i.e. $T = 1/t$, in which case equation (8.7) becomes

$$\hat{y}_t = a + bT \tag{8.8}$$

In this form the values of a and b can be evaluated using normal linear regression procedures (see Table 8.4 for road expenditure data application) such that calculated values and forecasts of the dependent variable $\hat{y}_t$ can be evaluated using equation (8.7) as is shown in Fig. 8.3. The forecast for 1978 ($t = 12$) is given by $\hat{y}_{12} = 1300.5 - 996.9/12 = 1217.4$.

For this particular form of the hyperbola it should be noted that for $b > 0$, $\hat{y}_t$ reduces as t increases and approaches the value a asymptotically. Such a curve might well fit a variable declining with time but declining to a fixed level not equal to zero.

98

TABLE 8.4. Calculations required to fit hyperbolic (i) curve to road expenditure data

Variable	Dependent	Independent
Form	y_t	$T = 1/t$

$n = 11$ $\Sigma y_t = 11295$ $\Sigma y_t^2 = 12997117$ $\Sigma T = 3.02$ $\Sigma T^2 = 1.56$ $\Sigma T y_t = 2382.3$

$$b = \frac{n \Sigma T y_t - \Sigma T \Sigma y_t}{n \Sigma T^2 - (\Sigma T)^2} = \frac{11(2382.36) - 3.02(11295)}{11(1.56) - (3.02)^2} = -996.9$$

$$a = \frac{\Sigma y_t - b \Sigma T}{n} = \frac{(11295) + 996.9(3.02)}{11} = 1300.5$$

therefore

$$\hat{y}_t = 1300.5 - 996.9/t$$

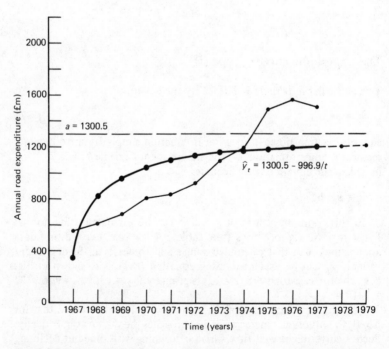

Fig. 8.3 Fitted hyperbolic (i) curve and forecasts for road expenditure data

TABLE 8.5. Calculations required to fit hyperbolic (ii) curve to road expenditure data

Variable	Dependent	Independent		
Form	$Y_t = 1/y_t$	$T = t$		
$n = 11$	$\Sigma Y_t = 0.01212$ $\Sigma Y_t^2 = 0.000015$	$\Sigma t = 66$ $\Sigma t^2 = 506$		$\Sigma tY_t = 0.0596$

$$b = \frac{n\Sigma t\, Y_t - \Sigma t\, \Sigma Y_t}{n\Sigma t^2 - (\Sigma t)^2} = \frac{11(0.0596) - 66(0.01212)}{11(506) - (66)^2} = -0.000119$$

$$a = \frac{\Sigma Y_t - b\Sigma t}{n} = \frac{(0.01212) + 0.00019(66)}{11} = 0.001816$$

therefore

$$\hat{y}_t = 1/(0.001816 - 0.000119t)$$

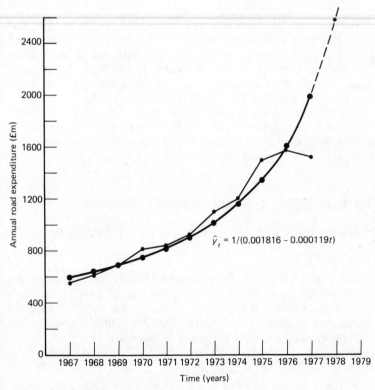

$$\hat{y}_t = 1/(0.001816 - 0.000119t)$$

Fig. 8.4 Fitted hyperbolic (ii) curve and forecasts for road expenditure data

For $b < 0$, $\hat{y}_t$ is only positive if $t > b/a$ and as t increases $\hat{y}_t$ also increases and approaches the value of a asymtotically.

This form of hyperbola could well fit a growth situation reaching saturation.

The hyperbolic curve – type (ii)

Another version of an hyperbola is defined by the equation

$$\hat{y}_t = 1/(a + bt) \tag{8.9}$$

This version of the hyperbola can be transposed into a linear equation by taking reciprocals of the dependent variable $\hat{y}_t$ rather than the independent variable t, as for the type (i) hyperbola. Thus if $Y_t = 1/y_t$, equation (8.9) becomes

$$\hat{Y}_t = a + bt \tag{8.10}$$

In this form the values of a and b can be evaluated using normal linear regression procedures (see Table 8.5 for road expenditure data application) such that calculated values of forecasts of the original (i.e. non-transformed) dependent variable $\hat{y}_t$ can be evaluated using equation (8.9) as shown in Fig. 8.4. The forecast for 1978 ($t = 12$) is given by $\hat{y}_{12} = 1/[0.001816{-}0.000119\,(12)] = 2577.3$.

For this particular form of the hyperbola it should be noted that for $b > 0$, $\hat{y}_t$ approaches zero as t increases but for $b < 0$, $\hat{y}_t$ approaches infinity as t approaches a value of a/b. This latter discontinuity is unlikely to reflect real life situations.

The hyperbolic – type (iii) or simple rational curve

Yet another version of the hyperbola is defined by the equation

$$\hat{y}_t = t/(a + bt) \tag{8.11}$$

This slightly more complex hyperbola which is also referred to as a simple rational curve can be transposed into a linear equation by taking reciprocals of both the dependent variable $\hat{y}_t$ (i.e. $\hat{Y}_t = 1/\hat{y}_t$) and the independent variable t (i.e. $T = 1/t$). When this double-reciprocal transformation is incorporated, equation (8.11) becomes

$$\hat{Y}_t = a'T + b' \tag{8.12}$$

In this form the values of a' and b' can be calculated using normal regression procedures (see Table 8.6) but remembering that in the

TABLE 8.6. Calculations required to fit hyperbolic (iii) curve to road expenditure data

Variable	Dependent	Independent
Form	$Y_t = 1/y_t$	$T = 1/t$

$n = 11$ $\Sigma Y_t = 0.01212$ $\Sigma Y_t^2 = 0.000015$ $\Sigma T = 3.02$ $\Sigma T^2 = 1.56$ $\Sigma T\, Y_t = 0.00426$

$$b' = \frac{n\Sigma T\, Y_t - \Sigma T\, \Sigma Y_t}{n\Sigma T^2 - (\Sigma T)^2} = \frac{11(0.00426) - 3.02(0.01212)}{11(1.56) - (3.02)^2} = 0.00127$$

$$a' = \frac{\Sigma Y_t - b\Sigma T}{n} = \frac{(0.01212) - 0.00127(3.02)}{11} = 0.000753$$

$$a = b' = 0.00127 \quad \text{and} \quad b = a' = 0.000753$$

therefore

$$\hat{y}_t = t/(0.00127 + 0.000753t)$$

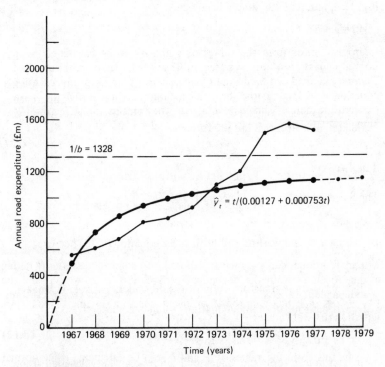

Fig. 8.5 Fitted hyperbolic (iii) curve and forecasts for road expenditure data

transformed model the roles of a' and b' are reversed, with b' taking the value of the intercept at $T = 0$ and a' representing the slope. Thus for equation (8.11) it follows that $a = b'$ and $b = a'$.

For the road expenditure data the best fitting hyperbola (iii) is shown in Fig. 8.5. The forecast for 1978 ($t = 12$) is given by $y_{12} = 12/[0.00127 + 0.000753(12)] = 1164$.

For this curve, irrespective of the polarity of b at $t = 0, \hat{y}_t = 0$. For positive values of b, $\hat{y}_t$ increases asymtotically to a value of $1/b$ as t increases. With b negative this curve, like the hyperbola (ii) curve, becomes unstable at time $t = a/b$.

The logarithmic curve

The logarithmic curve is defined by the equation

$$\hat{y}_t = a + b\log_e t \tag{8.13}$$

By taking natural logarithms of the independent variable t (i.e. $T = \log_e t$) equation (8.13) simply becomes

$$\hat{y}_t = a + bT \tag{8.14}$$

In this linear form the values of a and b can be calculated using normal regression procedures (see Table 8.7 for road expenditure data example). Calculated values and forecasts can then be produced using equation (8.13) and the best logarithmic curve fitting the road expenditure data is shown in Fig. 8.6, the forecast for 1978 ($t = 12$) being evaluated as $\hat{y}_{12} = 315.6 + 447 \log_e 12 = 1426$.

The S-curve

The S-curve is defined by the equation

$$\hat{y}_t = e^{a+b/t} \tag{8.15}$$

By taking natural logarithms of both sides, equation (8.15) becomes

$$\log_e \hat{y}_t = a + b/t \tag{8.16}$$

If a logarithmic transformation of the dependent variable $\hat{y}_t$ is taken ($\hat{Y}_t = \log_e \hat{y}_t$) and reciprocals of the dependent variable ($T = 1/t$), equation (8.16) becomes

$$\hat{Y}_t = a + bT \tag{8.17}$$

In this linear form the values of a and b can be calculated using normal regression procedures (see Table 8.8). Calculated values and

TABLE 8.7. Calculations required to fit logarithmic curve to road expenditure data

Variable	Dependent	Independent
Form	y_t	$T = \log_e t$

$n = 11$ $\Sigma y_t = 11295$ $\Sigma y_t^2 = 12997117$ $\Sigma T = 17.50$ $\Sigma T^2 = 33.40$ $\Sigma T y_t = 20454.1$

$$b = \frac{n \Sigma T y_t - \Sigma T \Sigma y_t}{n \Sigma T^2 - (\Sigma T)^2} = \frac{11(20454.15) - 17.5(11295)}{11(33.4) - (17.5)^2} = 447$$

$$a = \frac{\Sigma y_t - b \Sigma T}{n} = \frac{(11295) - 447(17.5)}{11} = 315.6$$

therefore

$$\hat{y}_t = 315.6 + 447\log_e t$$

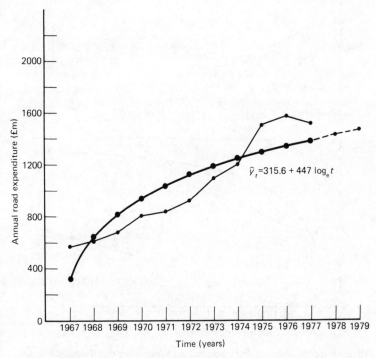

Fig. 8.6 Fitted logarithmic curve and forecasts for road expenditure data

TABLE 8.8. Calculations required to fit S-curve to road expenditure data

Variable	Dependent	Independent
Form	$Y_t = \log_e y_t$	$T = 1/t$

$n = 11$ $\Sigma Y_t = 75.60$ $\Sigma Y_t^2 = 520.91$ $\Sigma T = 3.00$ $\Sigma T^2 = 1.56$ $\Sigma T Y_t = 19.97$

$$b = \frac{n\Sigma T Y_t - \Sigma T \Sigma Y_t}{n\Sigma T^2 - (\Sigma T)^2} = \frac{11(19.97) - 3.02(75.60)}{11(1.56) - (3.02)^2} = 1.08$$

$$a = \frac{\Sigma Y_t - b\Sigma T}{n} = \frac{(75.60) + 1.08(3.02)}{11} = 7.169$$

therefore

$$\hat{y}_t = e^{(7.169 - 1.08/t)}$$

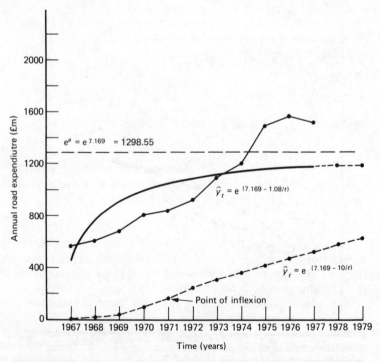

Fig. 8.7 Fitted S-curve and forecasts for road expenditure data (with additional true S-curve)

forecasts can then be derived from equation (8.15) and for the road expenditure data the resulting curve is shown in Fig. 8.7, the forecast for 1978 ($t = 12$) being given by $\hat{y}_{12} = e^{(7.169 - 1.08/12)} = 1186.8$.

In spite of its name, the S-curve only exhibits an S-shaped characteristic if the coefficient b is negative and greater in absolute value than a (i.e. $b < -a$).

Since for the road expenditure data $a = 7.169$ and $b = -1.08$, the resultant curve is not truly an S-shape. To demonstrate the S-curve characteristic an additional curve has been added to Fig. 8.7 with $a = 7.69, b = -10$.

When the curve $\hat{y}_t = e^{a+b/t}$ does exhibit a true S-shaped characteristic it is particularly useful since it can be used to represent the life cycle of service of a product. Such life cycles often follow a pattern of a slow start, a subsequent phase of steep growth and a final saturation phase (i.e. an asymptotic approach to a fixed saturation level (in this case e^a). Such a characteristic is true of many aspects of business and industry and particularly of technological developments. However, in practice the logistic or Gompertz curves (see Chapter 9) are more likely to provide a reasonable fit than the S-curve defined here. For this S-curve the point of inflexion, where growth rates greater than unity change to growth rates of less than unity, occurs at $t = -b/2$ which for $b = -10$ occurs at $t = 5$ (i.e. 1971).

The inverse log curve

The inverse log curve is defined by the equation

$$\hat{y}_t = 1/(a + b\log_e t) \tag{8.18}$$

By taking a reciprocal transformation of the dependent variable $\hat{y}_t$ (i.e. $\hat{Y}_t = 1/\hat{y}_t$) and a logarithmic transformation of the dependent variable t (i.e. $T = \log_e t$) equation (8.18) becomes

$$\hat{Y}_t = a + bT \tag{8.19}$$

In this linear form the values of a and b can be calculated using normal regression procedures (see Table 8.9) and the resulting curve for the road expenditure data is shown in Fig. 8.8, the forecast for 1978 ($t = 12$) being given by $\hat{y}_{12} = 1/(0.0019 - 0.000 \log_e 12) = 1592$.

The inverse logarithmic curve has not featured much in the forecasting literature and is included here mainly to complete the eight possible combinations of semi- and double-logarithmic and/or reciprocal transformations that can produce a linear equation. In fitting the road expenditure data, this curve is by no means the worst and although it must necessarily go negative if b is negative and if $a/b < \log_e t$. In this

TABLE 8.9. Calculations required to fit inverse log curve to road expenditure data

Variable	Dependent	Independent
Form	$Y_t = 1/y_t$	$T = \log_e t$

$n = 11$ $\Sigma Y_t = 0.01212$ $\Sigma Y_t^2 = 0.000015$ $\Sigma T = 17.50$ $\Sigma T^2 = 33.40$ $\Sigma T Y_t = 0.0163$

$$b = \frac{n\Sigma T Y_t - \Sigma T \Sigma Y_t}{n\Sigma T^2 - (\Sigma T)^2} = \frac{11(0.01636) - 17.5(0.01212)}{11(33.4) - (17.5)^2} = 0.000052$$

$$a = \frac{\Sigma Y_t - b\Sigma T}{n} = \frac{(0.01212) + 0.0005(17.5)}{11} = 0.00192$$

therefore

$$\hat{y}_t = 1/(0.00192 - 0.00052\log_e t)$$

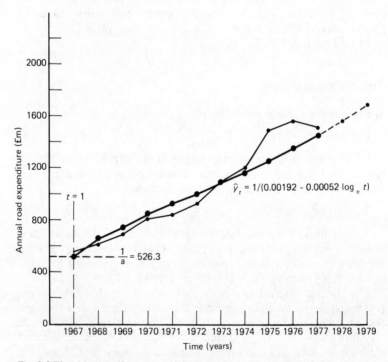

Fig. 8.8 Fitted inverse log curve and forecasts for road expenditure data

```
EXE-CURFT
CURFT

NEED HELP?N

TO BEGIN.....IS THE DATA IN A FILE,OR TO BE INPUT FROM
THE TERMINAL?(TYPE FIL OR TER)?FIL
WHAT IS THE NAME OF THE FILE?ROADS
HOW MANY OBSERVATIONS?11

                    LEAST SQUARES CURVES FIT

CURVE TYPE        INDEX OF        A              B
                  DETERMINATION

1. Y=A+(B*X)      .952827         366.273        110.091
2. Y=A*EXP(B*X)   .977491         496.694        .110739
3. Y=A*(X^B)      .883499         457.957        .468622
4. Y=A+(B/X)      .506134         1297.41        -985.639
5. Y=1/(A+B*X)    .963429         1.81829E-03    -1.19351E-04
6. Y=X/(A+B*X)    .727748         1.27423E-03    7.52365E-04
7. Y=A+B*LOG(X)   .793308         315.37         447.137
8. Y=EXP(A+B/X)   .616789         7.16906        -1.08057
9. Y=1/A+B*LOGX   .950259         1.94168E-03    -5.27611E-04


                    STANDARD ERROR ESTIMATES


CURVE TYPE        REGRESSION      INTERCEPT(A)   SLOPE(B)


1. Y=A+(B*X)      85.6381         55.3796        8.16527
2. Y=A*EXP(B*X)   5.87479E-02     1.03872        5.60140E-03
3. Y=A*(X^B)      .133655         1.10389        5.67235E-02
4. Y=A+(B/X)      277.092         122.141        324.54
5. Y=1/(A+B*X)    8.12943E-05     5.25706E-05    7.75111E-06
6. Y=X/(A+B*X)    2.21808E-04     2.59790E-04    9.77718E-05
7. Y=A+B*LOG(X)   179.259         132.568        76.0783
8. Y=EXP(A+B/X)   .242403         .10685         .283911
9. Y=1/A+B*LOGX   9.48091E-05     7.01144E-05    4.02373E-05
```

Fig. 8.9 Output of typical curve fitting computer program CURFT processing the road expenditure data held in a file named ROADS

particular case, however this does not occur until $t = 48$, which is well outside the time range for which forecasts might be made.

Choosing the appropriate curve for forecasting

Figure 8.9 shows a typical computer printout of a commercial curve fitting package applied to the road expenditure data. This package is typical of most curve fitting packages in that initially it fits several

```
MORE DETAILS FOR CURVE TYPE?(TYPE IN NUMBER OR 0 TO QUIT?2
   2. Y=A*EXP(B*X) IS AN EXPONENTIAL FUNCTION.  THE RESULTS
      OF A LEAST-SQUARES FIT OF ITS LINEAR TRANSFORM
      (SORTED IN ORDER OF ASCENDING VALUES OF X)
      ARE AS FOLLOWS:

PERIOD        Y-ACTUAL        Y-CALC        PCT DIFFER
1             560             554.859                .9
2             608             619.835       -1.9
3             685             692.42        -1
4             807             773.504                4.3
5             839             864.084       -2.9
6             914             965.271       -5.3
7             1100            1078.31                2
8             1196            1204.58       -.7
9             1499            1345.64                11.3
10            1574            1503.22                4.7
11            1513            1679.25       -9.9

FORECASTING AHEAD FOR 12 PERIODS
PERIOD        Y-CALC
12            1875.9
13            2095.57
14            2340.97
15            2615.11
16            2921.34
17            3263.44
18            3645.6
19            4072.51
20            4549.42
21            5082.17
22            5677.31
23            6342.14
```

Fig. 8.10 Output of CURFT when more details are required for the exponential curve

curves and subsequently it allows the user to choose one, or several of the curves to actually produce forecasts. This particular package recommends the choice of curve to be made using the highest value of the index of determination — which in this case would mean the exponential curve. Figure 8.10 shows that when more details of the exponential curve are required, the program produces actual and calculated values of y and forecasts for up to twelve periods ahead.

In choosing a curve with which to forecast, other measures such as the mean squared error (MSE) or mean absolute percentage error (MAPE) can be used, but the ranked order of selection does not alter greatly using these measures as opposed to the index of determination as can be seen in Table 8.10. It should be noted, however, that for true

TABLE 8.10. Summary of curve fitting performance to road expenditure data

Curve name	Index of determination	MSE	MAPE
(1) Linear	0.953 3	6000 2	6.36 2
(2) Exponential (simple)	0.977 1	5574 1	4.10 1
(3) Power	0.883 5	15749 4	10.54 5
(4) Hyperbolic (i)	0.506 9	62819 9	25.02 9
(5) Hyperbolic (ii)	0.963 2	23217 5	6.68 4
(6) Hyperbolic (iii) or simple rational	0.728 7	52351 7	17.25 7
(7) Logarithmic	0.793 6	26291 6	15.80 6
(8) S	0.617 8	54108 8	20.16 8
(9) Inverse logarithmic	0.950 4	9893 3	6.56 3

comparisons the index of determination r^2 (or the correlation coefficient r) should be based on untransformed data and not on transformed data as here, and in most computer curve fitting packages.

However, when selecting a curve for forecasting purposes one should always remember that fitting and forecasting are not the same thing. The overall characteristics of the curve should also be taken into account, particularly if it is known to be discontinuous.

As mentioned at the start of this chapter, some authors[1,5] would not consider it feasible to use curves based on transformations of the independent variable time, whereas others[3,4] consider such curves can be used in special circumstances.

Appendix E, which indicates the logic and calculations required to establish the regression coefficients a and b, can be used to establish the curve parameters a and b for all the curves described in this chapter if the transformations specified in Table 8.1 are taken.

References

1. I.C.I. (1964) *Mathematical Trend Curves. An Aid to Forecasting* Edinburgh, Oliver & Boyd
2. MEADOWS, D.H., MEADOWS, D.L. *et al.* (1972) *The Limits to Growth* London, Earth Island
3. WHEELWRIGHT, S.C. AND MAKRIDAKIS, S. (1978) *Forecasting Methods and Applications,* New York, Wiley/Hamilton
4. WHEELWRIGHT, S.C. AND MAKRIDAKIS, S. (1974) *Interactive Forecasting* Palo Alto, The Scientific Press
5. YEOMANS, K.A. (1968) *Applied Statistics – Statistics for the Social Scientist* Vol. 2, Harmondsworth, Penguin

Exercise

For the road vehicle expenditure data (page 91) confirm the values of the curve parameters a and b and correlation coefficients r as indicated below

Curve	a	b	r
Simple exponential	799.818	0.133696	0.970
Power	751.615	0.543226	0.885
Hyperbolic (i)	2555.65	−2146.15	0.612
Hyperbolic (ii)	0.001070	−0.000076	0.969
Hyperbolic (iii) or simple rational	0.000747	0.000408	0.777
Logarithmic	338.548	1023.12	0.806
S	7.81549	−1.19814	0.707
Inverse logarithmic	0.001127	−0.000323	0.928

Chapter 9

Curve fitting–curves that can be expressed by the modified exponential curve

Apart from the S-curve (and then only in very special circumstances – see page 105) all the curves considered in Chapter 8 fail to cope with situations where the rate of change of the slope of the curve being fitted changes. Such *points of inflexion,* where increasing rates of growth suddenly change to decreasing rates of growth, often occur where the data being analysed exhibit:

(i) an initial period of relatively slow, but gradually increasing growth;

(ii) an intermediate period of rapid growth followed by

(iii) a final period where the rate of growth declines and observed values approach a saturation level.

Such situations often occur in business and industry, particularly during the life of a product, and as such are referred to as 'life cycle curves'. Two curves which always have a point of inflexion and which will, therefore, be generally better at fitting life cycle situations are the Gompertz and logistic curves.

Both the Gompertz and the logistic curves can be derived from a curve known as the modified exponential curve, in much the same way as the curves considered in Chapter 8 were all derived from a straight line (i.e. linear curve). This chapter, therefore, will initially consider the fitting and forecasting procedures associated with the modified exponential curve and subsequently, by suitable transformation of the dependent variable y_t, consider the Gompertz and logistic curves. All three curves will be fitted to the road expenditure data (already considered in Chapters 7 and 8) to assist readers in checking any fitting procedures they might be developing themselves.

In general, because curves based on the modified exponential equation are defined by three parameters (as opposed to two parameters for those based on a straight line) they usually give a better curve fitting performance albeit at the expense of more calculations.

The three curves to be investigated in this chapter together with their equations, necessary transformations and basic shapes are shown in Table 9.1.

111

TABLE 9.1. Curves that can be transposed to a modified exponential curve by suitable transformation

Curve name	Equation	Transformations	Basic shape
Modified exponential	$\hat{y}_t = a + bc^t$	None	
Gompertz	$\hat{y}_t = a\,b^{c^{t}}$	$Y_t = \log y_t$	
Logistic	$\hat{y}_t = 1/(a + bc^t)$	$Y_t = 1/y_t$	

The response of these three curves to the road expenditure data are also recorded in Table 9.5 which indicates the rankings of the fitted performance of the curves in terms of mean squared error (MSE) and mean absolute percentage error (MAPE). Readers should note that the Gompertz and logistic curves both produce a better fitting performance than any of those described in Chapter 8, although this is obviously not always true.

The modified exponential curve

The modified exponential curve, which does not itself ever produce a point of inflexion, is defined by the equation

$$\hat{y}_t = a + bc^t \tag{9.1}$$

Because the values of three coefficients (a, b and c) are required to define this curve, the fitting of the modified exponential curve using the method of least squares discussed in Chapters 7 and 8 is no longer a simple or straightforward procedure. Whilst a least squares procedure known as the Gomes method is available, a much simpler procedure and one which in practice is just as effective is that recorded by Bryant[1]. It is this method which will be considered throughout this chapter.

Fitting the modified exponential curve

The basic theory underlying this fitting method is beyond the scope of this book but can be found in some statistics texts (e.g. Bryant[1],

p. 185). Essentially, the method defines c and then evaluates the other curve coefficients b and a.

Assuming the same time convention used throughout this book, namely that the first observation occurs at time $t = 1$ and also that $\Sigma = \displaystyle\sum_{t=1}^{n}$ unless otherwise stated, the equations defining the three coefficients of the modified exponential curves equation are, in order of computation

$$c = \frac{(n-1)\displaystyle\sum_{t=1}^{n-1} y_t\, y_{t+1} \quad - \quad \displaystyle\sum_{t=1}^{n-1} y_t \displaystyle\sum_{t=1}^{n-1} y_{t+1}}{(n-1)\displaystyle\sum_{t=1}^{n-1} y^2{}_t \quad - \quad \left(\displaystyle\sum_{t=1}^{n-1} y_t\right)^2} \tag{9.2}$$

$$b = \frac{n\,\Sigma\, c^t y_t \;-\; \Sigma c^t\, \Sigma y_t}{n\,\Sigma\, c^{2t} \;-\; (\Sigma c^t)^2} \tag{9.3}$$

$$a = \frac{\Sigma y_t \;-\; b\Sigma c_t}{n} \tag{9.4}$$

Table 9.2 indicates the necessary tabulations required to evaluate the parameters a, b and c for the modified exponential equation which best fits the road expenditure data considered in Chapters 7 and 8, together with the actual calculations involved as defined by equations (9.2), (9.3) and (9.4).

As a result of these calculations with $a = 4899$, $b = -4571$ and $c = 0.9728$, it follows that the modified exponential equation which best fits the road expenditure data is given by

$$\hat{y}_t = 4899 - 4571\,(0.97208)^t$$

and Fig. 9.1. indicates this curve's response and the two periods ahead forecasts, where the forecast for 1978 ($t = 12$) is given by

$$\hat{y}_{12} = 4899 - 4571\,(0.97208)^{12} = 1644.8$$

Whilst the modified exponential is generally regarded only as the basic equation from which the more useful Gompertz and logistic curves can be produced by suitable transformation of the dependent variable, it can in its own right provide a good fit and sensible forecasts in certain situations. When the launching of a new product produces a sudden upsurge of sales or demand, as might well occur with a well timed advertising campaign, because the initial period does not require the relatively slow response more suitably fitted by curves with an

TABLE 9.2. Complete statistics and calculations to fit a modified exponential curve to road expenditure data

Year	t	y_t	y_{t+1}	$y_t y_{t+1}$	y_t^2	c^t	$c^t y_t$	c^{2t}	$\hat{y}_t$
1967	1	560	608	340480	313600	0.97208	544.36467	0.94494	455.69
1968	2	608	685	416480	369664	0.94494	574.52296	0.89291	579.74
1969	3	685	807	552795	469225	0.91856	629.21098	0.84375	700.34
1970	4	807	839	677073	651249	0.89291	720.57827	0.79729	817.57
1971	5	839	914	766864	703921	0.86798	728.23491	0.75339	931.53
1972	6	914	1100	1005400	835396	0.84375	771.18333	0.71191	1042.30
1973	7	1100	1196	1315600	1210000	0.82019	902.20666	0.67271	1149.98
1974	8	1196	1499	1792804	1430416	0.79729	953.55650	0.63567	1254.65
1975	9	1499	1574	2359426	2247001	0.77503	1161.76634	0.60067	1356.40
1976	10	1574	1513	2381462	2477476	0.75339	1185.83371	0.56759	1455.31
1977	11	1513				0.73235	1108.05138	0.53634	1551.47
$\sum\limits_{t=1}^{n-1}$		9782	10735	11608366	10707948				
$\sum$		11295				9.31846	9279.50971	7.95716	

$$c = \frac{(n-1)\sum\limits_{t=1}^{n-1} y_t y_{t+1} - \sum\limits_{t=1}^{n-1} y_t \sum\limits_{t=1}^{n-1} y_{t+1}}{(n-1)\sum\limits_{t=1}^{n-1} y_t^2 - \left(\sum\limits_{t=1}^{n-1} y_t\right)^2} = \frac{10(11608366) - 9782(10735)}{10(10707948) - (9782)^2} = \frac{116083660 - 105009770}{107079480 - 95687524} = \frac{11073890}{11391956} = 0.97208$$

$$b = \frac{n \sum c^t y_t - \sum c^t \sum y_t}{n \sum c^{2t} - (\sum c^t)^2} = \frac{11(9279.50971) - 9.31846(11295)}{11(7.95716) - (9.3184.6)^2} = \frac{102074.6 - 105252.0}{87.530 - 86.833} = -\frac{3177.4}{0.695} = -4571$$

$$a = \frac{\sum y_t - b\sum c^t}{n} = \frac{11295 + 4571(9.31846)}{11} = 4899$$

Note: $\sum = \sum\limits_{t=1}^{n}$ unless otherwise stated.

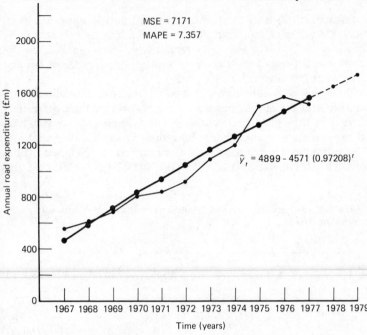

Fig. 9.1 Fitted modified exponential curve and forecasts for road expenditure data

S-shaped characteristic, the modified exponential can provide a good fit particularly if an asymtotic approach to some upper limit is required.

The Gompertz curve

The Gompertz curve is defined by the equation

$$\hat{y}_t = ab^{c^t} \tag{9.5}$$

Taking either natural logarithms or logarithms to base 10 of both sides of the equation one obtains

$$\log \hat{y}_t = \log a + c^t \log b \tag{9.6}$$

which becomes

$$\hat{Y}_t = a' + b'\, c^t \tag{9.7}$$

where

$$\hat{Y}_t = \log \hat{y}_t, \ a' = \log a \text{ and } b' = \log b$$

Equation (9.7) is in the form of a modified exponential equation, hence the values of the parameters c, b' and a' can be evaluated using equations (9.2), (9.3) and (9.4) respectively. Having established the value of c, a (= antilog a') and b (= antilog b'), calculated values and forecasts can be obtained using equation (9.5).

Table 9.3 gives summary statistics for the road expenditure data together with the calculations required to evaluate the three parameters of the best fitting Gompertz curve. In this example logarithms to base 10 have been used but obviously logarithms to any base will do. From these calculations it follows that the Gompertz curve which best fits the road expenditure data has paramenters $c = 0.93176$, $b = 0.0961435$ and

TABLE 9.3. Summary statistics and calculations to fit a Gompertz curve to road expenditure data ($Y_t = \log_{10} y_t$)

Summary statistics ($t = 1$ to 10)

$$\sum_{t=1}^{n-1} Y_t = 29.65129 \quad \sum_{t=1}^{n-1} Y_{t+1} = 30.08295 \quad \sum_{t=1}^{n-1} Y_t Y_{t+1} = 89.40335 \quad \sum_{t=1}^{n-1} Y_t^2 = 88.13835$$

$$c = \frac{(n-1)\sum\limits_{t=1}^{n-1} Y_t Y_{t+1} - \sum\limits_{t=1}^{n-1} Y_t \sum\limits_{t=1}^{n-1} Y_{t+1}}{(n-1)\sum\limits_{t=1}^{n-1} Y_t^2 - \left(\sum\limits_{t=1}^{n-1} Y_t\right)^2} = \frac{10(89.40335)-29.65129(30.08295)}{10(88.13835) - (29.65129)^2}$$

$$= \frac{894.0335 - 891.99827}{881.3835 - 879.19899} = \frac{2.033673}{2.18451} = 0.93176$$

Summary statistics ($t = 1$ to 11)

$$\Sigma c^t = 7.37932 \qquad \Sigma c^t Y_t = 21.77579 \qquad \Sigma c^{2t} = 5.19510 \qquad \Sigma Y_t = 32.83113$$

$$b' = \frac{n\Sigma c^t Y_t - \Sigma c^t \Sigma Y_t}{n\Sigma c^{2t} - (\Sigma c^t)^2} = \frac{11(21.77579) - 7.37932(32.83113)}{11(5.19510) - (7.37932)^2}$$

$$= \frac{239.53369 - 242.271414}{57.1461 - 54.45436} = \frac{-2.7377}{2.6917} = -1.01708$$

$$a' = \frac{\Sigma Y_t - b'\Sigma c^t}{n} = \frac{32.83113 + 1.01708(7.37932)}{11} = 3.66694$$

$$a = \text{antilog}_{10} \, a' = 4644.5 \quad b = \text{antilog}_{10} b' = 0.0961435$$

$$\hat{y}_t = 4644.5 \, (0.0961435)^{(0.93176)t}$$

a = 4644.5 such that the equation for calculated values and forecasts is given by

$$\hat{y}_t = 4644.5 \, (0.0961435)^{(0.93176)^t}$$

The forecast for 1978 (t = 12) is given by

$$\hat{y}_{12} = 4644.5 \, (0.0961435)^{(0.93176)^{12}} = 1703.8$$

Both calculated values for t = 1 to 11 and the two periods ahead forecasts, t = 12 and t = 13, are shown Fig. 9.2.

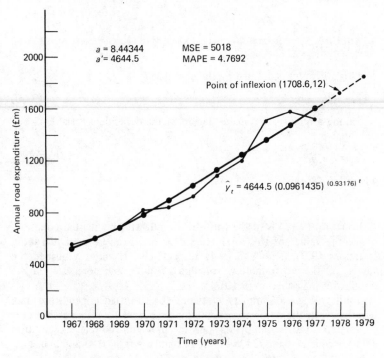

Fig. 9.2 Fitted Gompertz curve and forecasts for road expenditure data

As has already been stated, the Gompertz curve exhibits a typical S-shaped characteristic which is particularly useful in life cycle situations. Its point of inflexion occurs at time t_p where

$$t_p = \frac{1}{\log_e c} \log_e \left(\frac{-1}{\log_e b} \right) \tag{9.8}$$

at which time the value of the independent variable $\hat{y}_{t_p}$ is given by

$$\hat{y}_{t_p} = \frac{a}{e} \tag{9.9}$$

where e = 2.71828.

For the road expenditure data the values of t_p and $\hat{y}_{t_p}$ are 12.04 (i.e. 1978) and 1708.6 respectively and this point of inflexion is indicated in Fig. 9.2. At this point the growth per year reaches a maximum of 120 units and declines thereafter. Readers should note that in this case the point of inflexion does not occur within the sample data.

The logistic curve

The logistic curve is defined by the equation

$$\hat{y}_t = 1/(a + bc^t) \tag{9.10}$$

Taking a reciprocal transformation of the dependent variable $\hat{y}_t$ one obtains

$$\hat{Y}_t = a + bc^t \tag{9.11}$$

where

$$\hat{Y}_t = 1/\hat{y}_t$$

Equation (9.11) is in the form of a modified exponential equation, hence the values of the parameters c, b and a can be evaluated using equations (9.2), (9.3) and (9.4) respectively. Having established the values of these parameters, calculated values and forecasts can be obtained using equation (9.10).

Table 9.4 gives summary statistics for the road expenditure data together with the necessary calculations required to evaluate the three parameters of the best fitting logistic curve for the road expenditure data for which $c = 0.8734$, $b = 0.00187$ and $a = 0.000193$ and hence

$$\hat{y}_t = 1/[0.000193 + (0.000187)(0.8734)^t]$$

The forecast for 1978 ($t = 12$) is given by

$$\hat{y}_{12} = 1/[0.000193 + (0.00187)(0.8734)^{12}]$$

$$= 1781$$

Both calculated values for $t = 1$ to 11 and the two-period ahead forecasts are shown in Fig. 9.3.

TABLE 9.4. Summary statistics and calculations to fit a logistic curve to road expenditure data ($Y_t = 1/y_t$)

Summary statistics (t = 1 to 10)

$$\sum_{t=1}^{n-1} Y_t = 0.011463 \quad \sum_{t=1}^{n-1} Y_{t+1} = 0.010338 \quad \sum_{t=1}^{n-1} Y_t Y_{t+1} = 0.00001308 \quad \sum_{t=1}^{n-1} Y_t^2 = 0.00001455$$

$$c = \frac{(n-1)\sum_{t=1}^{n-1} Y_t Y_{t+1} - \sum_{t=1}^{n-1} Y_t \sum_{t=1}^{n-1} Y_{t+1}}{(n-1)\sum_{t=1}^{n-1} Y_t^2 - \left(\sum_{t=1}^{n-1} Y_t\right)^2} = \frac{10(0.00001308) - 0.011463(0.010338)}{10(0.00001455) - (0.011463)^2}$$

$$= \frac{0.0001308 - 0.0001185}{0.0001455 - 0.0001314} = \frac{0.000123}{0.000141} = 0.8734$$

Summary statistics (t = 1 to 11)

$$\Sigma c^t = 5.34228 \qquad \Sigma c^t Y_t = 0.006745 \qquad \Sigma c^{2t} = 3.052465 \qquad \Sigma Y_t = 0.012124$$

$$b = \frac{n\Sigma c^t Y_t - \Sigma c^t \Sigma Y_t}{n\Sigma c^{2t} - (\Sigma c^t)^2} = \frac{11(0.006745) - 5.34228(0.012124)}{11(3.052465) - (5.34228)^2}$$

$$= \frac{0.074195 - 0.06477}{33.5771 - 28.5399} = \frac{0.00943}{5.03716} = 0.00187$$

$$a = \frac{\Sigma Y_t - b\Sigma c^t}{n} = \frac{0.012124 - 0.00187(5.34228)}{11} = 0.000193$$

$$\hat{y}_t = 1/[0.000193 + 0.00187(0.8734)^t]$$

The logistic curve exhibits an S-shaped characteristic with its point of inflexion occurring at time t_p where

$$t_\mathrm{p} = \frac{1}{\log_e c} \log_e\left(\frac{a}{b}\right) \tag{9.12}$$

at which time the value of the independent variable $\hat{y}_{t_\mathrm{p}}$ is given by

$$\hat{y}_{t_\mathrm{p}} = 1/2a \tag{9.13}$$

For the road expenditure data the values of t_p and $\hat{y}_{t_\mathrm{p}}$ are 16.7 (i.e. 1984) and 2590.6 respectively. Although this point of inflexion

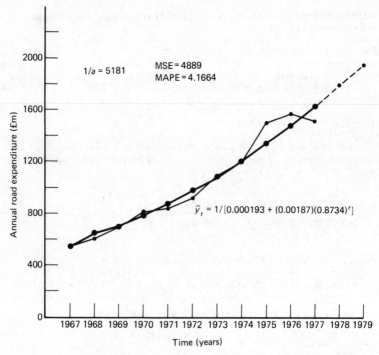

Fig. 9.3 Fitted logistic curve and forecasts for road expenditure data

does not come within the range of values plotted in Fig. 9.3, at this point of time the growth per year reaches a maximum of 175 units.

The fitting performance of the modified exponential, Gompertz and logistics curves in terms of mean squared error (MSE) and mean absolute percentage error (MAPE) is shown in Table 9.5. From this it

TABLE 9.5. Summary of curve fitting performance to road expenditure data

Curve name	MSE	MAPE (%)
Modified exponential	7171	7.36
Gompertz	5018	4.77
Logistic	4889	4.17

can be seen that both the Gompertz and logistic curves provide a better fitting performance than any of the curves considered in Chapter 8 (see Table 8.10).

References

1. BRYANT, E.C. (1960) *Statistical Analysis,* New York, McGraw-Hill

Bibliography

GILCHRIST, W. (1976) *Statistical Forecasting,* New York, Wiley
I.C.I. (1964) *Mathematical Trend Curves. An Aid to Forecasting* Edinburgh, Oliver & Boyd
WHEELWRIGHT, S.C. AND MAKRIDAKIS, S. (1978) *Forecasting Methods and Applications* New York, Wiley/Hamilton

Exercise

For the road vehicle expenditure data (page 91) confirm values of the curve parameters a, b and c and $\hat{y}_{12}$, the forecast for 1978, as indicated below:

Curve	a	b	c	$\hat{y}_{12}$ at $\tau=1$ or $t = 12$
Modified exponential	787.906	192.467	1.286739	4752.86
Gompertz	252.061	3.5331	1.071568	4549.43
Logistic	−0.000485	0.001626	0.932877	4512.09

Chapter 10

Monitoring medium-term forecasting systems (the V-MASK/CUSUM method)

Since, in general terms, medium-term forecasting systems are more expensive to operate than short-term systems, it is possible to monitor medium-term forecasts using a more sophisticated method than the smoothed error tracking signal method described in Chapter 4. One disadvantage of that method is that whilst it detects changes very effectively, it cannot pinpoint exactly when such changes occur. This disadvantage of the smoothed error method prevents it evaluating a post-change average or forecast. Both these disadvantages can be overcome using the CUSUM method described in this chapter.

Graphical methods of assessing when forecasts go out of control using cumulative sums of errors (CUSUMS)

One of the problems of detecting when forecasts go out of control in practice is that a sudden change that may have caused an out of control situation may not be apparent because of the naturally high degree of random variation (noise) that often can occur in industrial and business data. In such situations it is essential that the camouflaging effect of this noise should be removed to reveal the true situation. Consider the demand data shown in Fig. 10.1. Here it would appear that the average level of demand is approximately constant at 250 over the 60 time periods involved. However, in reality a sudden change occurs in the data

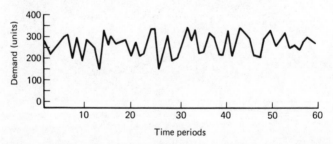

Fig. 10.1 Noisy data with an apparent average value of 250

122

in the 30th period when the average level changes by 8 per cent from 250 to 270. The reason that the reader cannot subjectively identify this change in average level is that it is obscured or camouflaged by the random variation or 'noise' of the data.

One method of removing the camouflaging effect of noise is to evaluate the cumulative sum of errors, known as the CUSUM. This is done by establishing a reference level or forecast, which in this case could be the assumed average sales level of 250, and subsequently evaluating the errors or differrences of the individual data values from this reference. This procedure will produce a series of positive and negative errors which can then be cumulated to produce the CUSUM. Any reader slightly confused by this explanation need only be reminded of the system of scoring adopted in the game of golf.

In golf a reference value is established which is known as 'par', this being the number of strokes per hole (and hence for the course) that a professional is expected to take. Scoring is then related to par and thus a 'birdie' indicates a score of one under par and a 'bogey' one over. Because such scores against par are cumulated, one player's performance can always be compared with another's irrespective of their relative positions on the course. Such a scoring method is far simpler and much more meaningful than one which is based on the total number of strokes taken.

Returning to the data of Fig. 10.1, if the cumulative sum of errors were to be formed using 250 as the reference value, and if the true average were indeed 250 one would expect the plot of the CUSUM to remain horizontal, simply because the effect of the positive and negative errors would be approximately equal and opposite and would, therefore, cancel out. Examination of the CUSUM plot for these data, using 250 as the reference value (Fig. 10.2) shows that the CUSUM

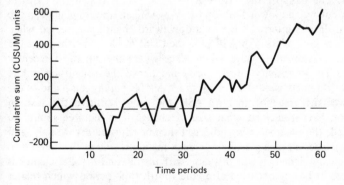

Fig. 10.2 CUSUM plot for noisy data with reference value set equal to 250

does indeed remain horizontal up to the 30th period, thus confirming that the average value during that time was indeed 250. After the 30th period, however, one cannot fail to see that the CUSUM no longer remains horizontal but starts to climb steeply. This must mean that the positive errors now exceed negative errors, indicating that the reference value after the 30th period must be below the actual average and one can assume therefore that an upward change must have occurred. Since the rate of climb of the CUSUM plot must be an indication of by how much positive errors exceed negative errors cumulatively, measurement of this rate of climb must indicate the actual size of change. In this case the rate of climb is 20 units per period, indicating that using 250 as the reference the size of the change is 20 and, hence, the average level of demand per period must be 270 units from the 30th period onwards.

Where data are being presented graphically, a CUSUM presentation will give a much better indication of when changes in data occur since:
(i)   the camouflaging effect of noise present in the data is removed;
(ii) the scale is enlarged; and
(iii) the sizes of any changes are easily measured.

The V-MASK/CUSUM test

Whilst the use of graphical CUSUM presentations is most useful for subjectively highlighting changes or discontinuities in data, for consistent detection of changes of a certain magnitude and particularly the timing of such changes the method needs to be extended. Figure 10.3 shows the CUSUM plot for the out of control forecasting situation where the forecast is fixed at 90. Superimposed on this CUSUM plot is a V-MASK whose pivot is placed b periods ahead of the current or most recent point on the CUSUM plot, and angled at a/b units per time period. The basis of the V-MASK/CUSUM test is that if the CUSUM plot is cut by the lower limb of the V-MASK an upward change in the original data is inferred whereas a downward change is detected when the upper limb of the V-MASK cuts the CUSUM plot. In either case the change is assumed to have taken place where the cut most recently occurs. The sensitivity of the test, and hence the magnitude of the change it detects is controlled by the V-MASK parameters a and b; the narrower the angle of the V-MASK the more sensitive the test. In practice, having decided what size of change it is required should be detected, the parameters a and b can then be adjusted accordingly, and the construction of a plastic or perspex mask also allows the method to be easily implemented. In this case with $a = 20$ and $b = 2$ a change is detected as having occurred after the fourth time period which relates sensibly to what has occurred to the true demand. Because the timing

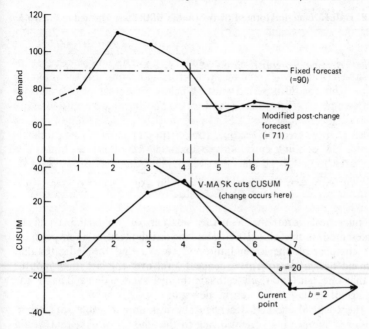

Fig. 10.3 Out of control forecasting situation with associated CUSUM plot with superimposed V-MASK

of the change has also been identified, it is possible also to evaluate a post-change forecast of 71 units, this being the average of demand values occurring subsequent to the change.

Numerical interpretation of the V-MASK/CUSUM test

Examination of Fig. 10.3 indicates that the V-MASK test (in numerical terms) is essentially a test examining the values of S_i (the sum of the i most recent forecasting errors) against some linear limits L_i. Expressing these limits in terms of b (the number of periods ahead) at which the V-MASK is pivoted and a (the parameter controlling V-MASK's half-angle) these limits can be expressed as:

$$L_i = \pm \frac{a}{b}(i + b) \qquad (10.1)$$

where, in this case, $a = 20$, $b = 2$ and i represents the number of periods back from the current point; and hence, for this situation:

$$L_i = \pm 10\,(i + 2) \qquad (10.2)$$

TABLE 10.1. Numerical form of the V-MASK/CUSUM test depicted in Fig. 10.3.

				Sum of i most recent errors						
Period	Demand	Forecast	Error	S_1	S_2	S_3	S_4	S_5	S_6	S_7
1	80	90	−10	−10						
2	110	90	20	20	10					
3	105	90	15	15	35	25				
4	95	90	5	5	20	40	30			
5	68	90	−22	−22	−17	−2	18	8		
6	74	90	−16	−16	−38	−33	−18	2	−8	
7	71	90	−19	−19	−35	−57*	−52	−37	−17	−27
	$L_i = 10(i + 2)$			±30	±40	±50	±60	±70	±80	±90

In numerical form the V-MASK analysis of Fig. 10.3 could be represented as in Table 10.1. Here, the last demand value in period 7 is seen to break the lower limit − L_3 at S_3, and this indicates that demand has *fallen* to a new demand level over the last three months so that one can tentatively estimate the new average demand as 71, the average of the last three months' demand.

The CUSUM method described above is impracticable for a computerized monitoring system owing to the amount of data that would necessarily be stored. Harrison and Davies[1] have, therefore, proposed a modified form of the CUSUM technique which is suitable as a computerized monitoring system and this method is now described in detail.

V-MASK/CUSUM test in a form suitable for automatic computation

The V-MASK/CUSUM test described in the preceeding section can be expressed in a form suitable for computer implementation using the two equations

$$D_t = \min (D_{t-1}; a) + \left(\frac{a}{b} + e_t\right) \qquad (10.3)$$

and

$$R_t = \min (R_{t-1}; a) + \left(\frac{a}{b} - e_t\right) \qquad (10.4)$$

where a and b are the V-MASK parameters, e_t is the current or most recent forecasting error, and min $(D_{t-1}; a)$ is interpreted as meaning take the value of D_{t-1} (the previous value of D_t) or a (the V-MASK

TABLE 10.2. Numerical form of V-MASK/CUSUM analysis suitable for computer implementation

Period	Demand	Forecast	Error	$(a|b-e_t)$	$min(R_{t-1}; a)$	R_t	$(a|b+e_t)$	$min(D_{t-1}; a)$	D_t
1	80	90	−10	20	20*	40	0	20*	20
2	110	90	20	−10	20	10	30	20	50
3	105	90	15	−5	10	5	25	20	45
4	95	90	5	5	5	−10	15	20	35
5	68	90	−22	32	10	42	−12	20	8 $\left.\right\}$ D_t
6	74	90	−16	26	20	46	−6	8	2 $\left.\right\}$ <20
7	71	90	−19	29	20	49	−9	2	−7*

*Initial assumption

parameter) whichever is the smaller. The test is interpreted such that if either D_t or R_t go negative a change is detected (equivalent to the V-MASK cutting the CUSUM) which started in the preceeding period when whichever value of D_t or R_t became less than a. If D_t goes negative, a reduction in the average value of the original data can be assumed whereas when R_t goes negative an increase can be assumed. Table 10.2 shows the application of this test to the data considered earlier in Fig. 10.3 where the forecast is fixed at 90 and the V-MASK is defined by $a = 20$ and $b = 2$. From Table 10.2 it can be seen that a downward change is detected in period 7 when D_t goes negative and that this change occurred in period 5 when D_t became less than $a = 20$. This result confirms the earlier findings of Table 10.1.

The computational ease with which this Harrison and Davies version of the V-MASK/CUSUM test can be implemented is demonstrated in Fig. 10.4, a printout from a TI59 programmable calculator, which replicates the example already considered in both Tables 10.1 and 10.2.

For simplicity, throughout the explanation of the V-MASK/CUSUM test it has been assumed that the forecast remains fixed. However, since it is the errors that form the CUSUM, the method can be used irrespective of the forecasting model being used and is therefore suitable with all the models discussed in this book.

In practice, although it may appear a trifle naive to operate a forecasting system which assumes that the forecast is fixed at one value until there is evidence to suggest (i.e. as indicated by a V-MASK/CUSUM test) that a different fixed value would be more appropriate, such a system does have particular advantages. This is especially true in manufacturing industries where production schedules are linked to forecasts and the changing of such schedules should be kept to a minimum.

Selection of the V-MASK parameters a and b

It is apparent that the V-MASK/CUSUM test depends totally on the selection of the V-MASK parameters a and b. Although there is no standardized, simple method of selecting a and b, in practice this does not appear to have been an insuperable problem in getting the method adopted. Given that a size of change is specified for a particular time series, by plotting the cumulative sum of errors and pivoting a V-MASK b periods ahead, and then narrowing the half-angle of the V-MASK until one of its limbs just cuts the CUSUM plot; this procedure will define the appropriate value of the second V-MASK parameter a.

A slightly more sophisticated method[3] is to develop a computer

V-MASK/CUSUM test 1

		A	
	20.		
		B	
	2.		
		REF	
	90.		
Period			
	80.	———————— Demand	
	40.	———————— R_t	
1	20.	———————————D_t	
	110.		
	10.		
2	50.		
	105.		
3	5.		
	45.		
	95.		
4	10.		
	35.		
	68.		
5	42.		
	8.	——————— $D_t < a$	
	74.		
6	46.		
	2.		
	71.		
7	49.		
	−7.	——————— $D_t < 0$	
	3.	NO	
	71.	$\overline{x}$	

Fig. 10.4 Printout from a TI59 program for the V-MASK/CUSUM test

SUMMARY

Run No	Changes detected	A for V-mask	Statistical info		
			MSE	MAPE	BIAS
1	4	24.4	53.8363	15.7524	1.75101E-06
2	5	14.0544	40.5944	13.4921	2.50144E-07

B for V-MASK = 2 FOR ALL RUNS

NOMINATE RUN REQUIRED 1 TO 2   71

DETAILED SUMMARY

Run No	Change number	Begins-data PT	Mean or reference	Size of change	Confidence level %
1	****	START	33.25	****	
	1	5	49.5	16.25	93.7808
	2	9	23.6667	25.8333	94.4283
	3	12	42.2	18.5333	99.9775
	4	47	28	14.2	99.9998

Fig. 10.5 Computer printout of V-MASK/CUSUM analysis of sales pattern with irregular pattern (Fig. 10.6) showing intermittent average levels

program which in applying the V-MASK/CUSUM test to a time series progressively reduces the half-angle of the V-MASK until the number of changes identified can be sensibly interpreted in the original series. Figure 10.5 shows the output of such a program where with b fixed at a value of 2 when a = 24.4, four changes are identified and when a is reduced to a value of 14.0544, five changes are found. Figure 10.5 also indicates that with an initial average value of 33.25, the starting point of each of the four changes on run no. 1 occurred at periods 5, 9, 12 and 47 between which the average (i.e. forecast) values were 49.5, 23.6667, 42.2 and 28 respectively – all significantly different to the preceeding average value or forecast. Figure 10.6 shows these average values superimposed on the original sales data in what is known as a Manhatten diagram.

Although more complicated and more expensive to operate than the smoothed error monitoring method, because the V-MASK/CUSUM monitoring method can determine exactly when a change occurs, a post-change average or forecast can be estimated.

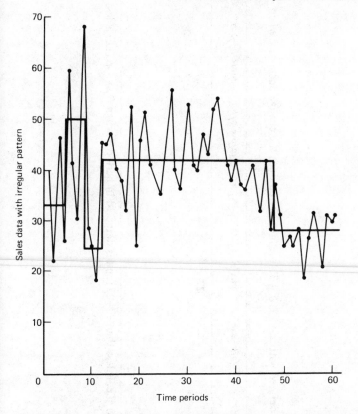

Fig. 10.6 Sales data with irregular pattern and superimposed Manhatten diagram

Reference

1. HARRISON, P.J. AND DAVIES, O.L. (1964) 'The use of cumulative sum (CUSUM) techniques for the control of routine forecasts of product demand', *Operations Research*, **12**, 325

Bibliography

BS5703 (1980) *Data Analysis and Quality Control using Cusum Techniques*, British Standards Institution
LEWIS, C.D. (1980) 'The use of a computerised V-mask to identify small changes in process means', *Quality Assurance*, **6**, 3
WOODWARD, R.H. AND GOLDSMITH, P.L. (1964) *Cumulative Sum Techniques*, I.C.I. monograph No. 3, Edinburgh, Oliver & Boyd

Exercise

Complete the table below using a V-MASK defined with $a = 27$, $b = 3$. In which period does the change occur and when is it detected?

Period t	Observed data	Forecast	Error	$(a/b - e_t)$	$\min(R_{t-1}; a)$	R_t	$(a/b + e_t)$	$\min(D_{t-1}; a)$	D_t
1	107	100			27			27	
2	94	100							
3	110	100							
4	92	100							
5	116	100							
6	121	100							
7	123	100							

The change occurs in period 5 when $R_t = 20$ (i.e. is less than $a = 27$) and is detected in period 7 when $R_t = -6$ (i.e. is less than zero).

Appendices

Figure A.1

Flow diagram to evaluate

(i)   exponentially weighted average forecast (with optional Σe_t term);
(ii) adaptive response rate forecast;
(iii) delayed adaptive response rate forecast.

Figure A.2

Flow diagram to evaluate Brown's adaptive smoothed forecast

Figure A.3

Flow diagram to either establish seasonal pattern with at least four seasons of data, or update seasonal pattern with single observation

Figure A.4

Flow diagram to evaluate

(i)   sum of squared errors
(ii)   mean squared error
(iii) mean error
(iv)   mean absolute percentage error
(v)   mean percentage error

$$\Sigma = \sum_{t=0}^{n-1}$$

Figure A.5

Flow diagram to establish coefficients of regression a and b and calculated values and forecasts $\hat{y}_t$

Figure A.6

Flow diagram to establish parameter of modified exponential curve and calculated values and forecasts $\hat{y}_t$

133

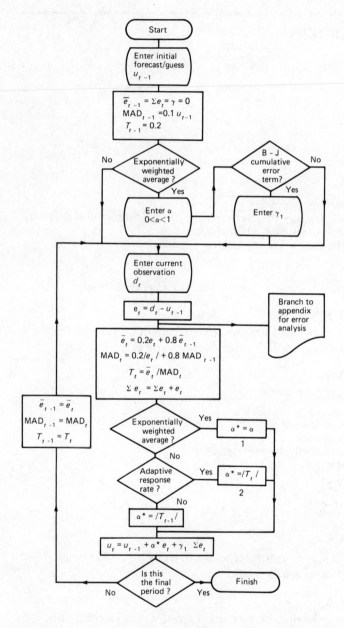

Fig. A.1

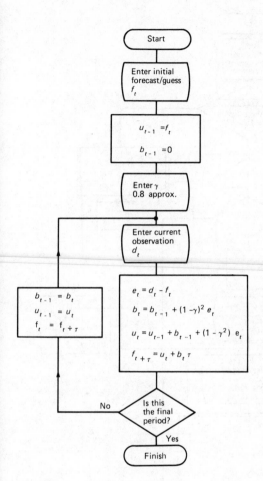

Fig. A.2

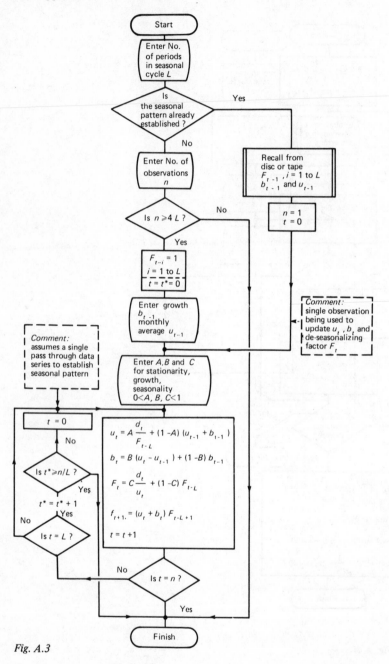

Fig. A.3

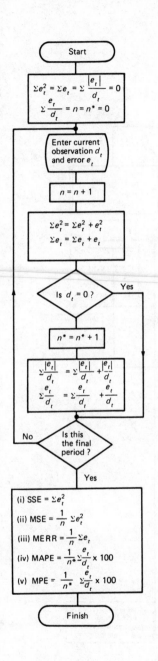

Fig. A.4

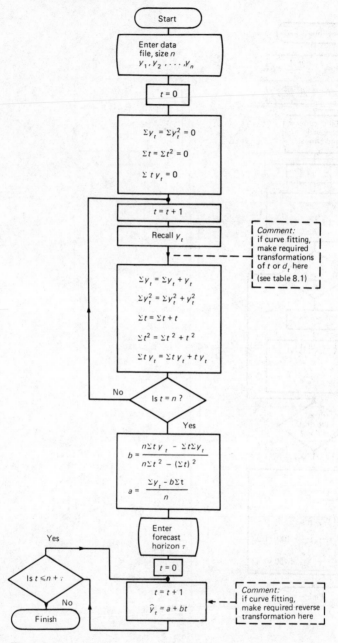

Fig. A.5

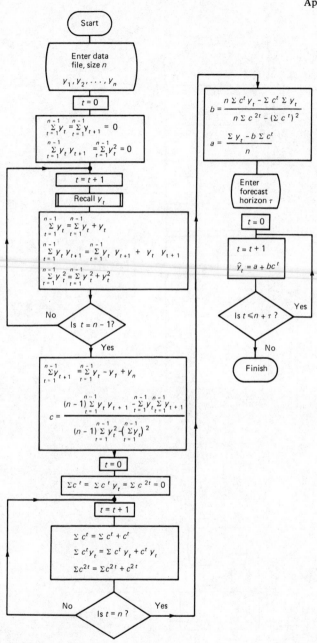

Fig. A.6

Index